THE **AT WAR** SERIES

USS IOWA AT WAR

KIT & CAROLYN BONNER

ZENITH
PRESS

First published in 2007 by Zenith Press, an imprint of MBI Publishing Company LLC, Galtier Plaza, Suite 200, 380 Jackson Street, St. Paul, MN 55101-3885 USA

Zenith Press titles are also available at discounts in bulk quantity for industrial or sales-promotional use. For details write to Special Sales Manager at MBI Publishing Company, Galtier Plaza, Suite 200, 380 Jackson Street, St. Paul, MN 55101-3885 USA.

To find out more about our books, join us online at www.zenithpress.com.

Editor: Steve Gansen
Designer: Jennie Maass

Printed in China

Library of Congress Cataloging-in-Publication Data

Bonner, Kit, 1945-
  USS Iowa at war / Kit Bonner and Carolyn Bonner.
    p. cm.
  Includes bibliographical references.
  ISBN-13: 978-0-7603-2804-0 (softbound)
  ISBN-10: 0-7603-2804-8 (softbound)
  1. Iowa (Ship)—History. I. Bonner, Carolyn. II. Title.
VA65.I59B66 2007
359.3'252—dc22

                    2006023619

On the front cover: The USS *Iowa* (BB-61) opens fire with a full main and secondary battery broadside to starboard. Nine 16-inch 50-caliber guns with six 5-inch 38-caliber guns in the secondary unit fire at a target in this July 1984 image. If armor-piercing shells were being used, the combined weight of the 16-inch and 5-inch shells fired was 12.3 tons. The main battery had a range of 24 miles at 45 degrees elevation, whereas the 5-inch gun fired up to ten miles. *U.S. Navy*

Inset: The USS *Iowa* sits serenely in a reserve fleet row in the Suisun Bay Reserve Fleet anchorage off Benicia, California. The ship has weathered, and the pristine gray paint job has become dull. However, this is only cosmetic and can be reme-

died with about a hundred thousand gallons of primer and paint. Aside from being anchored to the bottom of the bay, the *Iowa* is moored abreast of the ex–USS *Proteus* (AS-19). It was lengthened by 44 feet to accommodate Polaris missiles and their successors. The *Proteus* was often anchored in Holy Loch, Scotland, to allow ballistic missile submarines in need of replenishment and repairs to remain close to their patrol areas. *Author's Collection by Sarah Lanzaro*

On the frontispiece:
Iowa-class battleships have their 16-inch main battery trained to port. Astern of the two battleships is the nuclear cruiser USS *Long Beach* (CGN-9), a *Spruance*-class destroyer, and bringing up the rear is a *Knox*-class frigate. The majestic and brute-like power of the *Iowa*-class battleships is shown. Aside from the pre–World War II–designed 16-inch 50-caliber guns, the *Iowa* class now sported modernized armored Tomahawk launchers; four 20mm CIWS mounts for a last-ditch stand against incoming missiles, suicide boats, and heavy-caliber shore-battery projectiles, and Harpoon antiship missiles. The electronics suite of World War II was upgraded, and a combat engagement center was added. *U.S. Navy*

On the title pages:
Photograph taken in July 2002, just three months after the *Iowa* arrived at the Suisun Bay Reserve Fleet. The *Iowa* was and is a popular attraction among the "ghost fleet" vessels, and amateur photographers are always being run off by security forces. The exclusion zone is 500 yards, yet another visitor is even more difficult to force out of the exclusion zone. Fishermen know that the biggest fish hide among the moored ships; the anglers must catch them before *they* are caught. *Author's Collection*

On the back cover:
The USS *Iowa* inbound to her homeport of Norfolk, Virginia, on April 5, 1985. Her starboard crane is out and prepared to receive fuel. It appears as if most of the crew that is not on duty is out on the bridge watching as the ship returns home. This is an excellent view of three of the four 20mm Phalanx CIWS "last-ditch-stand" guns that would protect the "Big Stick," as the *Iowa* was nicknamed. *U.S. Navy*

About the Authors:
Kit and Carolyn Bonner are naval historians and photographers. They have authored or co-authored numerous books, including *Great Ship Disasters*, *Warship Boneyards*, *Cold War at Sea*, and *Great Naval Disasters*. Kit was the naval consultant for the 1997 blockbuster film, *Titanic*. They live in Ione, California.

CONTENTS

The *USS* Iowa *at War* is dedicated to all those who fought so valiantly during the twentieth century aboard U.S. battleships:

1914: Tampico–Veracruz Incidents, Mexico
1941: Neutrality Patrol, North Atlantic
December 7, 1941: Pearl Harbor
October 26, 1942: Battle of Santa Cruz Island
November 1942: North Africa
November 14–15, 1942: Naval Battle of Guadalcanal
November 15, 1942: Battle of Savo Island
1943–1945: Bombardment of Japan and Japanese-occupied islands in the Pacific
1944: Bombardment of German positions in Normandy and southern France
1944–1945: Actions off the Philippines and Okinawa versus the kamikazes
1951–1953: Bombardment of North Korean positions
1969: Bombardment of North Vietnamese positions
1991: Persian Gulf War bombardment

And to the USS *Iowa* and the forty-seven who lost their lives in Turret No. 2 on April 19, 1989.

FOREWORD

THOMAS J. VILSACK
GOVERNOR

OFFICE OF THE GOVERNOR
STATE CAPITOL
DES MOINES, IOWA 50319

SALLY J. PEDERSON
LT. GOVERNOR

For years, Iowans have been filled with pride to know that one of the greatest battleships ever to sail the seas carries the name of their home state. The USS *Iowa* defended the shores of our country for over half a century from tyranny, and preserved the liberties and freedoms that all Americans hold dear. It has come to be more than just a battleship, but a symbol of the strength and ideals for which this state, and this nation, stand.

It is fitting this class of warships be named after a state that boasts a long and proud tradition of service and sacrifice. Our citizens have always been eager to answer the call to defend our nation's freedoms and way of life. One Iowa family in particular embodied this spirit in a very real, yet tragic way.

Following the attack on Pearl Harbor, America sent out a call for young men to defend our country. Five young brothers, all born and raised in Waterloo, Iowa, answered that call. The Sullivan family of Waterloo gave all five of their boys to the Navy, and together they proudly set off together protect our country. On Friday, November 13, 1942, Japanese submarines torpedoed the USS *Juneau*, sinking it and killing over 680 members of the crew, including all five Sullivan brothers.

Historians refer to the Sullivan brothers and their fellow servicemen as members of the "Greatest Generation," a generation of Americans who put the good of their country, of their communities, before their own interests and lives. It was an era of selfless acts for noble causes in which families like the Sullivans made unimaginable sacrifices. Yet one should never assume the following generations have not lived up to such greatness. The spirit of service and sacrifice has been passed down through every generation and can be seen in many Iowans today.

In the rotunda of the Iowa State Capitol sits a large replica of the USS *Iowa* seen by thousands of visitors each year. Additionally, a large painting of the USS *Iowa* proudly hangs in my office conference room. Both are powerful images: the battleship symbolizes the great strength of our nation, while its sailors embody the sacrifice that makes that strength possible.

Now, more than sixty years after the USS *Iowa*'s first engagement in war, we, as a nation, are still fighting to protect the freedoms and way of life that brave men and women fought for in World War II and the conflicts thereafter. We will continue to honor their sacrifices, and always remember that we too, whether we face war or peace, must all do our part, and make our own sacrifices, for the greater good and for a brighter tomorrow.

Sincerely,

Tom Vilsack
Governor of Iowa

Looking aft from the anchor ground tackle in this January 2006 photo, it is possible to see what the sun, rain, and exposure will do to any vessel over a three-year period. The once well-polished teakwood decks have rotted in several areas, and standing water has resulted in rust pits and streaks. Valves are corroded shut, and any unsealed or untreated area is doomed to destruction. However, the huge 16-inch 50-caliber guns can be seen to good effect, and an American flag was later raised to celebrate the patriotism of this ship and the forty-seven men who died in Turret No. 2. Turret No. 2 is the three-barrel turret superfiring over the main deck 16-inch turret. *Author's Collection*

The *Iowa* has just cast off from the *Sea Victory* after a forty-four-day tow from Newport, Rhode Island. The trip was generally uneventful, and one of the authors was permitted to board the *Sea Victory* just inside the Golden Gate. Unfortunately, the prior stop had been in Panama, and exiting the *Sea Victory* was difficult—he did not have a passport or any method of proving that he had boarded the tow vessel in the Bay area. After endless questions, he was released. The *Iowa* behaved well, and the *Sea Victory* managed a steady 4.5 to 6.0 knots while under tow. The only complaint was the unbearable humidity in the Panama Canal region. *Author's Collection*

CHAPTER ONE
HISTORY

It was a beautiful spring day on April 21, 2001, as the USS *Iowa* (BB-61) was being towed through San Francisco Bay up to San Pablo Bay toward its anchorage in Suisun Bay, California. Hundreds of military, commercial, and pleasure ships make their way through this channel and up the American River every year, but this was a special ship. It was the flagship of the last active battleship class, and it had just traveled nearly six thousand miles over a period of forty-four days from Newport, Rhode Island, to its new home in the Suisun Bay Reserve Fleet. Thousands of well-wishers lined the shores of the San Francisco Bay Area route, as the huge, 887-foot-long, 58,000-ton ship moved by at six knots under tow by the oceangoing tug *Sea Victory*.

Finally, opposite the city of Benicia, the silent battleship was cast loose from the *Sea Victory*; harbor tugs warped it into place amongst the seventy-six famous, barely known, and unknown ships that make up the reserve fleet. A few of these ships date back to World War II, and now another of that era had joined their ranks.

Within months, its shiny gray paint began to oxidize, and small rust streaks appeared. By the end of the year, the battleship had taken on the patina of a reserve-fleet ship and was just another ship awaiting its fate. Only occasionally would a private yacht cruise by the anchorage (remaining outside the five hundred–foot security zone) to show its passengers the last battleship—for a fee, of course.

By early 2006, rain, sunlight, and bad weather had given this once beautiful ship to substantial surface rust. Burmese teakwood decks were rotting, and pools of water were eating away at hundreds of corners on the main deck. However, the damage was cosmetic, and the *Iowa* was merely in need of sandblasting, primer, paint, and new deck planking (high-grade Douglas fir) to bring it back to better days. Over 2005 and 2006, the U.S. Navy, which is still the legal owner, contracted for surface repairs to maintain the ship in presentable condition. The repairs did not include the hull and the ship's major systems, as they are in excellent working order. Of course, paint and new wooden planking are not sufficient to bring the *Iowa* into fighting trim. The price tag for seeing this beautiful ship again slicing through the sea at thirty knots would be several million dollars, and there would need to be a pressing call to arms for this type of warship.

An aft or stern view of the *Iowa* taken in the summer of 2003. The funnels are capped to prevent water from draining into the compartment below. The mast was shortened to allow the ship to be towed under several bridges in the San Francisco Bay area. Part of the mast can be seen off the aft deck on the helicopter pad. A helicopter landing area was outlined on the deck for a LAMPS III helicopter (SH-60B Sikorsky Sea Hawk). As there was no hangar facility, the permanent assignment of an air detachment did not occur. The helicopter was a visitor and not a permanent resident. Early in the career of the *Iowa* class, the battleships carried three fixed-wing aircraft in the form of an OS2U Kingfisher and later a faster and more capable Curtiss SC-1 Seahawk. Two aircraft were mounted on the two catapults, and a spare was carried. They were catapulted from the ship and retrieved by the huge derrick mounted aft on the ship's centerline. *Author's Collection*

As of early 2006, the navy was still carrying the USS *Iowa* on its register as a "category B" mobilization asset. In other words, it could be refurbished and put to sea to fight America's enemies in a very short time. Although at the time of this writing, this sixty-three-year-old battleship is still available for future naval warfare, that warfare will have no place for the battleship.

FUTURE NEED FOR BATTLESHIPS
In reality, the possibility of the *Iowa* or any of its three sister ships—the USS *New Jersey* (BB-62), USS *Missouri*

(BB-63), and USS *Wisconsin* (BB-64)—being recalled to active service is nil. Heavy-gun-duel sea warfare has passed into history, and the *Iowa* will soon be donated to a city or region that can support a museum ship of this size and monetary appetite.

Its three sisters have already found homes as memorial/museum ships. The *Missouri* is anchored within yards of the USS *Arizona* at Pearl Harbor; the *New Jersey* is in Camden, New Jersey; and the *Wisconsin* now calls Norfolk, Virginia, its home. These huge armored ships have joined an elite fraternity of U.S. Navy battleship memorials that also includes the *Arizona, Utah, Alabama, Massachusetts, North Carolina*, and the dowager queen, the *Texas*. No other nation pays such great homage to its battleships and its navy as the United States. The battleship is now a historical piece of naval hardware, and the majority of the international naval community recognized this fact just after the end of World War II.

After the U.S. Navy decided that the *Iowa* could be donated to a worthy city, various organizations had six months to vie for the ship as a museum piece. The process, like all federal programs, is complicated and difficult. In essence, an organization can compete for a warship if it satisfies a variety of regulations, such as having a realistic maintenance plan, adequate financial resources and reserves to keep the ship in museum-quality condition, as well as a business plan to ensure that the ship's preservation continues into the distant future. More importantly, the *Iowa* will require sufficient dockage, and the city or region must agree to preserve the ship in a patriotic and respectful way. The navy is very attentive to the care these battleships are given and has strict guidelines for museum ships. After all, many of these ships fought bravely and suffered damage as well as casualties. The American public's devotion to its military veterans requires nothing less. In addition, these ships are among the most expensive

The USS *Missouri* (BB-63) is moored in Pearl Harbor, Oahu, Hawaii. The *Missouri* was towed from Bremerton, Washington, via Astoria, Oregon, to its present site in early 1998. Soon after being decommissioned for the last time on March 31, 1992, after its successes in the Gulf War, the *Missouri* ended up at Bremerton's Inactive Ship Maintenance Facility. The *Sea Victory* towed the battleship to Astoria first so that microorganisms that had attached themselves to the hull could be killed by the fresh water of the Columbia River. This achieved, the *Missouri* went to sea at the end of a thick cable, and on June 22, 1998, it pulled by Diamond Head and into Pearl Harbor. Six months later, the Bristol fashion battleship, now moored just yards from the USS *Arizona* was opened to the public. It has been a very successful museum and a wonderful adjunct to the naval history of Pearl Harbor. Like bookends to World War II, the USS *Arizona* marks the beginning and the *Missouri* signifies the end. *U.S. Navy*

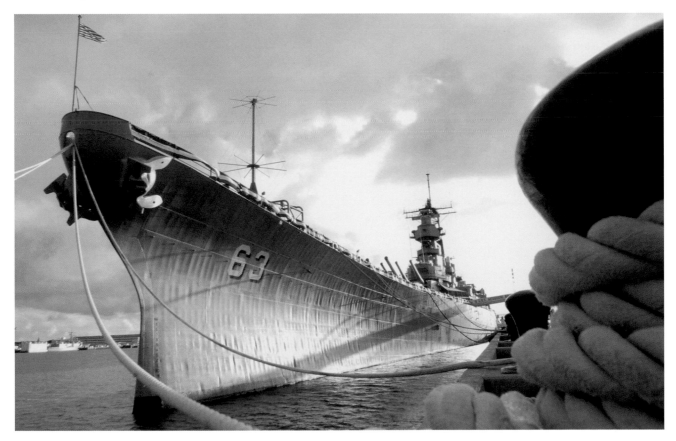

The USS *Alabama* moored in a purpose-built shallow pond in Mobile Bay, Alabama, in 2002. Unfortunately, the late 2005 hurricanes did substantial damage to the *Alabama* Museum, and heeled the battleship over to port about 5 degrees. Currently, the ship has been put back on an even keel, and repairs are proceeding on the pavilion and other aspects of the museum. The *Alabama* has been a museum ship since 1964. Ironically, the *Alabama* is one of the four *South Dakota*-class battleships upon which the *Iowa*-class design was based. *Author's Collection*

assets owned by the people of the United States, and the taxpayers expect proper care.

The USS *Iowa* fought valiantly in World War II, the Korean Conflict, and the Cold War against the Soviet bloc navies. It also participated in the "tanker wars" in the Persian Gulf by protecting the vital supply of oil to the world. Its record in war and peace is enviable and honorable.

Unfortunately, during peacetime, on April 19, 1989, a great tragedy aboard the *Iowa* caused the death of forty-seven men. The ship was involved in an exercise, dubbed FLEETEX 3-89, in the Caribbean. While test firing its forward battery of 16-inch guns, the ship suffered a "flareback" in Turret No. 2. A flareback is akin to a serious flash of combustibles, yet there is no explosion. Only fortune smiling on this ship prevented it from vaporizing. Had the flareback reached the lower shell and powder magazine, the ship would have suffered the same fate as the USS *Arizona* did when a Japanese aerial bomb blew up its forward half on December 7, 1941. That bomb exploded in the forward ammunition and powder magazine, causing an enormous explosive eruption that destroyed the entire ship. The explosion was caught by an amateur movie photographer and is one of the best-known images of World War II and the twentieth century.

The navy is not about to allow the *Iowa* and the

memory of those killed aboard her to be put in any hands that would not provide a long-term home and adequate financial support.

THE IOWA CLASS: THE EPITOME OF BATTLESHIP DESIGN

The battleship *Iowa* was also the namesake and prototype of the finest class of battleships the world has ever seen or ever will see. Naval architects, historians, and officers from all navies who have had the opportunity to visit these ships agree on a single tenet: that the *Iowa* class was the best ever built, and possessed an unmatched combination of great offensive fire power, excellent armor protection, and unbelievable speed. In all, the world's navies built over 250 battleships or battleship-type warships. The U.S. Navy contributed 95 ships, from the monitors and coastal battleships to the *Iowa*-class ocean-going battleship. Ironically, the one-hundred-year history of the battleship included a very small number of significant clashes between these giants. Nations did not rise or fall based on "blue-water" victories or defeats by dueling battleships.

At a time when the naval strength of a maritime nation was measured by the size and number of its operational battleships and how technologically advanced they were, the ultimate battleships were the *Iowa* and its three sisters. This strength was closely tied

An artist's conception of the USS *Iowa* located at the navy's former base at Rough and Ready Island, Stockton, California. The Port of Stockton is competing with a private group from San Francisco (not endorsed by the City and County of San Francisco) to acquire the *Iowa* as a centerpiece for a naval museum. The Port of Stockton offers a 90,000-square-foot warehouse that can easily be converted to a covered museum for extensive exhibits, meetings, and such. Just behind the proposed location of the ship is the relatively unknown but vital communications center for all submarines in the Pacific during World War II. There is a tremendous amount of naval history in the region, and many warships and auxiliaries were built in the Stockton area during the Second World War. *Port of Stockton*

to diplomatic power and international influence. Sending a battleship to a troubled area signified that a nation considered the difficulty grave and that an immediate resolution was necessary. Great Britain, the United States, Germany, and others sent battleships or pocket battleships into Spanish waters in 1936 and 1937 to help resolve or exacerbate the Spanish Civil War, depending on where their sympathies lay.

Less than a decade later, the Japanese surrendered to the Allies on the deck of the USS *Missouri*. The use of the *Missouri* for this ceremony was no accident: it was vital to impress the Japanese delegates with the raw power of the United States. An *Iowa*-class battleship was ideal for the task. Just months later, the "Mighty Mo" was once again used in a show of force, applying pressure to Communist elements threatening Greece and Turkey.

The *Iowa*-class battleship was not just new, but also downright novel. As war clouds began to develop over Europe in the late 1930s, the U.S. Navy approved the concept of a fast battleship (33 knots; 58,000 tons dis-

placement) with a main battery consisting of nine 16-inch 50-caliber guns that could lob a 2,700-pound projectile over twenty-five miles. The winning design was the six-ship *Iowa* class in April 1938. The ships were to be named for states: *Iowa*, *New Jersey*, *Missouri*, *Wisconsin*, *Kentucky*, and *Illinois*.

Of course, it was not simply the onset of World War II that caused the *Iowa* class to be approved and built; events leading up to its development began nearly two decades before World War II. The world's naval powers formally agreed to successive naval-arms limitation treaties beginning four years after the armistice that ended World War I. Like the nuclear-arms limitation treaties of the 1970s, a half-century later, in the 1920s the world sought to limit future war by reducing and equalizing the nations' battleship inventories, the super weapons of the era.

In 1922, the victorious Allied powers, including the United Kingdom, Italy, France, and Japan, sent diplomatic and naval representatives to Washington, D.C., at

The famous (or infamous) image of the flareback in turret two aboard the USS *Iowa* on April 19, 1989, some three hundred miles from Puerto Rico in the Caribbean. A flareback is like a box of matches igniting at once in a giant flash. However, in the case of the *Iowa*, the flash consumed all of the oxygen in the turret and literally asphyxiated the entire gun crew of 47 men. They were dead within a second. The center barrel powder bags split and allowed propellant charges (small pellets) to spill out in the powder bag and projectile loading tray. This was a recipe for immediate disaster. Had the flash propellant exploded or gained access to the lower magazine, the forward one half of the ship would have vaporized—like the explosion that consumed the battleship USS *Arizona* in the Japanese air attack on Pearl Harbor in 1941. The aft section of the ship would have quickly sunk, and it would have consumed years to determine the cause, and the foes of the battleship who cried that its technology was too ancient for the new age of electronics would have triumphed. Interestingly, this same type of accident occurred previously aboard the USS *Mississippi* (BB-41) in the same turret and barrel on two dates, June 12, 1924, and November 20, 1943. *U.S. Navy*

the invitation of the American government. The meeting centered on establishing building and overall naval strength ratios. In a few short months, the diplomats hammered out arrangements, and publicly, they appeared pleased with their efforts. After all, the United Kingdom was near bankruptcy and, with the United States, was vitally concerned about Japanese aims in the Pacific. A formula to curb capital-ship construction and naval growth put the brakes on Japanese ambitions, and allowed the United Kingdom a financial recovery period.

Most of the signatory nations clandestinely violated the original treaty before the ink was dry on the paper, and periodic meetings to reaffirm naval-arms limitations soon became pro forma. Finally, in 1936, the Japanese mission walked out of the London conference and openly defied the international community's restrictions on naval construction. The Imperial Japanese Navy had already embarked on a world-class aircraft carrier–building program. It was modernizing its battleships and, more importantly, had become free to build

The Imperial Japanese delegation aboard the USS *Missouri* (BB-63) on the day that Japan formally surrendered to the victorious Allies. These gentlemen, as representatives of the current Japanese government, were empowered to sign the unconditional surrender documents to be laid out on a plan table by General of the Armies Douglas MacArthur. This was an instance, among many, where the overwhelming power and majesty of a battleship was necessary to overpower the nation's enemies. It was on September 2, 1945, and the early morning ceremony took but twenty-three minutes to conclude. By 0930, the Japanese delegation had boarded their transportation craft for shore. The following day, the USS *Missouri* left for Pearl Harbor and then the United States. *U.S. Navy*

three of five projected *Yamato*-class battleships. These were the largest, most heavily armed battleships ever to put to sea. At approximately 73,000 tons, the *Yamato*s mounted nine 18.1-inch guns in their main battery plus twelve 6.1-inch guns in their secondary battery. Using six powder bags of propellant, the 18.1-inch guns could fire a phenomenal, 3,200-pound armor-piercing projectile over twenty-six miles with a moderate degree of accuracy. Added to this unparalleled firepower were scores of anti-aircraft weapons, seven floatplanes, and armor plating as thick as 25 inches. These giants consumed millions of precious skilled-work hours, incredible financial reserves, and resources that might have been better spent on aircraft carriers, submarines, and escort craft. Of the

five ships authorized, the *Yamato*, *Musashi*, and *Shinano* were built, although in 1944 the *Shinano* was redesigned as an 800-foot-long, 64,000-ton aircraft carrier. The fourth ship, known as *No.111* (unnamed), was laid down in 1940; work on it progressed until 1942, then stopped as the shipyard shifting its priorities to repair and smaller ship construction. The fifth ship, *No.797*, was stillborn, with a design but no contract.

The Japanese navy was overly supportive of the battleship and went beyond the *Yamato* class. Unbelievably, the Imperial Japanese Navy flirted with a two-ship super-*Yamato* class that would have displaced close to 80,000 tons and mounted six 20-inch guns in its main battery. The super-*Yamato* ships, identified as

A cutaway drawing of the USS *Iowa* (BB-61) gives a detailed look at the primary working areas of the *Iowa*-class battleship. *U.S. Navy*

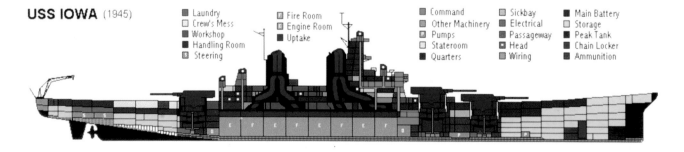

USS IOWA (1945)

■ Laundry	■ Fire Room	■ Command	□ Sickbay	■ Main Battery
□ Crew's Mess	■ Engine Room	■ Other Machinery	■ Electrical	□ Storage
■ Workshop	■ Uptake	▨ Pumps	▨ Passageway	▨ Peak Tank
■ Handling Room		□ Stateroom	▨ Head	■ Chain Locker
▨ Steering		■ Quarters	□ Wiring	■ Ammunition

The world's largest and most powerful battleship—the *Yamato.* This ship mounted nine 18.1-inch guns and could fire 3,200-pound armor-piercing shells twenty-six miles. With a full broadside, the *Yamato* and its sister the *Musashi* could fire a total of 28.8 tons of explosives. If a ship was on the receiving end of this broadside, it would be blown out of the water. Fortunately, this never happened, and both of these superbattleships were dispatched by American aircraft carrier bombers and torpedo planes. It took 120 minutes of bombing, and ten air-launched torpedoes to sink the *Yamato*—which had taken hundreds of thousands of hours to build over a more than two-year time. By the time these monsters went to sea, their time and value to the Imperial Navy had passed into history. It was now the turn of the aircraft carrier and the attack submarine to command the oceans. *Imperial Japanese Navy*

After absorbing one thousand-pound bomb after another plus ten well placed aerial torpedoes, the *Yamato* exploded in a fireball more than one thousand feet high. Within seconds after an American flier snapped this image, the *Yamato* disappeared beneath the sea. The end of the superbattleship had come, and now the *Iowa* class was the largest and most powerful on Earth. *U.S. Navy*

An artist's conception of the USS *Montana*. Aside from drawings and models, this was as far as this class ever got. World War II came to an end before there was a need for such a battleship class, and when the state of the Japanese navy became known, it definitively decided that any battleships beyond that of the *Iowa* class would be superfluous. *U.S. Navy*

No. 798 and *No. 799*, were planned and partially designed for the 1942 building program, yet no contracts were ever signed.

The Japanese navy's devotion to increasingly larger battleships was ironic in view of the wildly successful attack by British carrier-based torpedo bombers on the Italian navy moored at Taranto in November 1940 (three battleships sunk); severe American battleship losses (at Pearl Harbor, December 7, 1941: eight battleships sunk or damaged); and the triumphant Japanese navy air attack on the Royal Navy's HMS *Prince of Wales* and HMS *Repulse* (two battleship-type ships sunk). On December 10, 1941, the Japanese 22nd Naval Air Group sunk the *Repulse* and *Prince of Wales* in less than ninety minutes. This was a significant air victory over seemingly adequate antiaircraft defenses aboard ships maneuvering at high speeds on the open sea. The argument that it was easy to sink only ships tethered at anchor or moorings in a confined harbor was no longer valid. It seemed that every theater of naval warfare was experiencing battleship losses from naval aviation or submarines. Even near Salamis in Greece, the Luftwaffe sunk two antiquated Greek battleships on April 10, 1941.

The lesson was obvious, but it would take the sinking of the *Musashi* and *Yamato* by American naval aircraft in 1944 and 1945 respectively to drive home the point that airpower had trumped the battleship. Then the *Shinano* was sunk by an American submarine, the USS *Archerfish*, on November 29, 1944. This carrier had been prepared for sea trials a mere ten days earlier, and due to the rush of wartime, the watertight doors had yet to be installed. The *Archerfish*'s torpedo damage caused unrestrained flooding, and the ship quickly sank. In essence, all three of the *Yamato*-class battleships were quickly dispatched and provided no real value to the Imperial Japanese Navy.

However, the *Yamato* class and the specter of these monsters sinking Allied warships served as an impetus for the U.S. Navy to move forward on the *Iowa* class. Perhaps the primary value of the *Yamato* class was that it pushed the Allies to close the "battleship gap" between themselves and the Axis.

Work on the first four ships of the *Iowa* class proceeded quickly. There were six ships approved and funded: the *Iowa, New Jersey, Missouri, Wisconsin, Illinois,* and *Kentucky*. Not all of the *Iowa* class was completed by the end of World War II. In the autumn of 1945, the *Illinois* was 22 percent complete when work stopped, and the *Kentucky* was 73 percent complete when it was suspended. Parts from these ships were employed on the other four *Iowas*, and their propulsion machinery was installed in the fast replenishment ships USS *Sacramento* (AOE-1, commissioned March 14, 1964) and USS *Camden* (AOE-2, commissioned May 29, 1965). Six decades after the engineering plants were initiated, both fast-combat support ships have now been decommissioned, having served the navy well.

THE MONTANA CLASS: WOULD-BE SUCCESSOR TO THE IOWA CLASS

In the immediate postwar years numerous battleship admirals and other senior officers refused to acknowledge the fact that the fast carrier had become the world's new capital ship. With the vast number of ship types

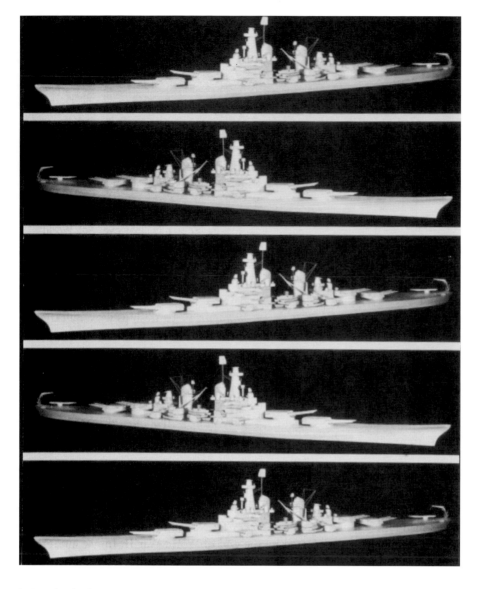

Models of the *Montana* class that were displayed during World War II to help sell the naval and political brass that the U.S. Navy was in dire need of several super-*Iowa* class battleships. The sales pitch fell on deaf ears when the surrender document was signed. Perhaps the models are somewhere in a dusty museum or a mislabeled crate in an Arlington or Washington, D.C., warehouse. *U.S. Navy*

being built during wartime, it was somewhat easy to convince the Pentagon to conceptualize and then build the five-ship *Montana* class. After all, the *Iowa* class was no match for the Japanese *Yamato* class; a still-more-powerful dreadnought was required for absolute national security.

The *Montana* class, at 890 feet in length, with a 70,500-ton full load, would have added a fourth three-barrel, 16-inch 50-caliber turret and certainly would have been something for Japan to contend with had it ever come to fruition. In reality, the war was being won with the *South Dakota, North Carolina,* and *Iowa* battleship classes, not to mention the primary weapons of naval aviation and attack submarines. And the *Montana* class would have sacrificed speed, down from the *Iowa*

class's 33 knots to 28 knots on 172,000 horsepower. Further, the *Montana*'s 120-foot, 8-inch beam would not allow this class to transit the Panama Canal, as the maximum width in the locks is 110 feet.

On the plus side, the *Montana*s would have introduced a secondary battery of twenty modern 5-inch 54-caliber guns that fired a 70-pound projectile 14.7 miles (compared to its popular predecessor, the 5-inch 38-caliber gun used aboard prior battleships, as well as destroyers, cruisers, and auxiliaries, which fired a 54-pound shell 9.8 miles). The antiaircraft battery of the *Montana*s also would have included 126 20mm and 40mm automatic cannons, as compared to the *Iowa* class's combined 137 guns of those types and the *South Dakota* class's 145.

The USS *Iowa* (BB-61) at sea off the Virginia Capes. The *Iowa* is steaming at moderate speed, and based on the armaments shown (20mm CIWS and armored Tomahawk and Harpoon launchers) the time period is after 1985. Despite being conceived in the late 1930s, the *Iowa* is a magnificent warship. The *Nimitz*-class aircraft carriers may be larger, but there is something stately and powerful about the *Iowa* class. *U.S. Navy*

As with the immediate battleship classes, the five ships of the *Montana* class would have been named for states. At the outset, the approved ships would have been the *Montana, Ohio, Maine, New Hampshire,* and *Louisiana.*

Aside from the increased displacement, the addition of another three-barrel, 16-inch turret, and the increased armor, the *Montana* class was not unlike the *Iowa* class, except that the *Iowa* class could steam at 33 knots, thus ensuring that the *Iowa*s could keep pace with the modern fast carriers, cruisers, and destroyers. This speed was a key design attribute of this class. Despite being considered only a marginally fast battleship, the *Montana* class was taken seriously. Yet the end of World War II ultimately stopped all but the most vital shipbuilding. Another battleship class was definitely not considered vital.

Inconceivably, the battleship devotees did not give up. Hard on the heels of the *Montana* class was one final concept. Certain U.S. Navy diehard battleship devotees began planning a future, unnamed battleship that would displace 106,500 tons and have an overall length of 1,160 feet. The main battery would be twelve 16-inch 50-caliber guns in four turrets. This design was never taken beyond the preliminary discussion stages, which was fortuitous: even four of these behemoths would have consumed enough resources to build fifteen *Essex*-class aircraft carriers. (Another motivation for battleship construction in general was the advancement of senior officers' careers. Fewer battleships meant fewer senior officers could pin on the stars of a rear admiral.)

The Royal Navy built a final battleship, the HMS *Vanguard*, as World War II was winding down, but it was scrapped a few years after the war concluded. By 1960, virtually every navy had broken up all of its older battleships, and only the Soviet Union and United States maintained battleships as potential weapons. In the final analysis, the *Iowa* and its three sisters were the world's last surviving superbattleships.

The USS *Michigan* (BB- 27) at speed. This 453-foot-long ship that displaced 16,000 tons was the American "dreadnought" like its sister, the *South Carolina*. They mounted eight 12-inch 45-caliber guns as their main armament and, superior to the British design, the turrets superfired, thus allowing a broadside of the entire main battery. Unfortunately, the *South Carolina* class utilized an obsolesent engine—the vertical triple expansion, and could only expect 18 knots at full speed. It is now generally recognized that the American design for the "dreadnought" pre-dated its British cousins. *U.S. Navy*

The HMS *Dreadnought* soon after being introduced to the world. The warship, which employed turbine propulsion and a main battery of ten 12-inch guns was revolutionary. The designers did away with multitudes of smaller weapons and calibers, and concentrated on a massive and powerful main battery. In addition, the *Dreadnought* had four screws and could make 21.6 knots—outdoing any battleship-type ships of the day. Besides, the name *Dreadnought* came to signify the dividing line in warship design eras. Anything built before 1906 was simply obsolete. *U.S. Naval Institute*

CHAPTER TWO

BATTLESHIPS: ICONS OF THE SEA

At the end of the Sino-Russian War in 1905, the international naval community had no choice but to include Japan. This development was a stunning change from the age-old European dominion over the seas. Fascinated, the world stood by and took note of the Japanese war machine after it smashed the Russian naval fleet at the Battle of Tsushima on May 28, 1905 and ended the czar's designs in the Pacific. The climatic naval engagement also firmly ensconced Japan in the naval superpower club. It was nearly inconceivable that this small island nation without any real natural resources, which had only just opened its frontiers to the United States and then other nations, had defeated the Russian bear. (U.S. president Theodore Roosevelt settled the war, with the combatants agreeing to the Treaty of Portsmouth on August 29, 1905.) However, there was no denying the tactical and strategic thought process that the Japanese Empire and its naval leadership had demonstrated. Japan purchased much of its naval hardware from Great Britain, and its ships looked distinctly like those of the Royal Navy; yet how they were deployed against the Russian forces was of greater value than the hardware.

As Japanese shipbuilding capacity developed, so did the number of warships emerging from indigenous yards. And Japanese naval officers took every opportunity to study western ways. It was not unusual for Japanese naval officers to be enrolled in the United States' finest universities as well as those in Great Britain. Isoroku Yamamoto, who was born in 1884 and became a career naval officer, examined and studied the American way, with emphasis on its resolve in the face of adversity. He attended Harvard University and was the naval attaché in Washington, D.C., from 1925 to 1928. He spoke of a sleeping giant and warned militarist hotheads in Japan that a war with the United States could only end in defeat. He was ignored, and so were the warnings of other naval theorists who observed the American navy and way of life. Yamamoto rose to command the Combined Fleet of the Japanese navy; however, his wise counsel bought Japan only six months of deceptive victories against the U.S. Navy from December 1941 to June 1942. The fact that men of Yamamoto's caliber were studying in the United States and observing the Americans should have been a tip-off as to Japanese plans. As the years went by, this society became

The American battleship USS *Nebraska* (BB-14). This is an example of a pre–dreadnought that was made obsolete by the concept of HMS *Dreadnought*. This was ironic, as it was commissioned after the HMS *Dreadnought*, and thus was regarded as just another armored ship. *Author's Collection*

virtually closed to the outside world. The only hints of Japanese ideas and plans were discovered accidentally; consequently, Europe watched the efforts of the Japanese naval machine with intense interest.

However, there were other issues to be considered beyond Japanese aims in the Pacific. With the Sino-Russian war settled, the international diplomatic and naval community moved on to something more interesting.

The real drama was about to take place in Great Britain, and it centered on a new and dynamic type of warship: the dreadnought. This revolutionary ship was built from keel up in fourteen months, which is still a record in the field of shipbuilding. Despite the fact that it was built in Great Britain, whose navy took the lion's share of the credit for the design and construction, the dreadnought was inspired by an article written by an Italian warship designer and specialist, Cuniberti, who recommended a ship that displaced 17,000 tons and had a main armament of twelve 12-inch guns and a speed of 24 knots. First Sea Lord Jackie Fisher of Great Britain's Royal Navy had thoughts along the same lines and ordered the construction of a modified version of Cuniberti's design: the ship named the HMS *Dreadnought*.

Although in March 1905 the United States considered and blueprinted an even more progressive concept with the designs that produced the USS *Michigan* (BB-27) and USS *South Carolina* (BB-26) in 1910, the Royal Navy stole a march on the world with its introduction of the HMS *Dreadnought* in December 1906. The HMS *Dreadnought*'s design unwittingly set the standard for the following century of battleship and battleship-type construction. Dubbed a "superbattleship," the HMS *Dreadnought* became the starting point for the true battleship, and all previous battleships became known as predreadnoughts. This new type of warship was one of the first to use steel armor and quadruple-screw propulsion. It employed the turbine as its propulsion and thus could make 21.6 knots. All previous ships used the vertical triple- or quadruple-expansion engines, which were now obsolete. Most of the armored warships could sustain 16, 18, or even 19 knots from their power plants, yet 21.6 knots was a rarity. Soon oil would take the place of coal as fuel, and earn the undying gratitude of the ship's crew, as coaling a ship was the filthiest job in any navy.

The *Dreadnought* design called for all big guns of the same caliber—a tremendous advantage. Fully loaded,

A year after the Armistice was signed that ended World War I, eleven relatively new battleships in the Philadelphia Navy Yard have been stripped of any useable material, and now await the scrapper's torch. Even the USS *Iowa* (BB-4) is in a back row and will soon be cut up. They were victims of the new dreadnought type and the end of hostilities. By this time, the dreadnought was also obsolete, as strides were being made every day to improve the battleship of tomorrow. *U.S. Navy*

The battleship USS *Texas* (BB-35) sits placidly near the Houston Ship Channel as part of the San Jacinto Battlefield Memorial. The ship is in an inlet cut out in La Porte, Texas, and nearly two hundred thousand people visit it every year. Aside from a very few older ships in other countries, the *Texas* is the only true throwback to another age in naval combat, a dreadnought as well as a ship of the line. Some sailors had to sling hammocks nightly, and the toilet facilities are reminiscent of those found in wilderness Federal Parks. The ship is beautifully cared for by a loving staff who know their craft and battleships.
Author's Collection

the ship displaced 17,900 tons, and it mounted ten 12-inch (305mm) guns in five double-barrel turrets. A broadside could consist of up to eight 12-inch guns, but could not bring all of the main battery to bear, since two of the forward turrets were wing mounted. In this respect the American versions of the dreadnought, the USS *Michigan* and USS *South Carolina*, were superior. Their turrets were superfiring: that is, they were arranged in pairs along the centerline, and one turret was higher than, and able to fire over, the other. However, the *Michigan* and *South Carolina* did not employ turbine power. At this stage, no design was perfect.

The advantage of the all-big-gun warship was the range of the main-battery shells compared to those of a secondary battery. If there was space aboard a warship, the consensus was that the largest single-caliber weapons should be mounted in the greatest numbers. Considering the effective range of the newer torpedoes, it did not behoove a captain to bring his ship in close proximity to the enemy. The Royal Navy's 12-inch weapon had a relatively accurate range of 14,000 yards, and a dreadnought-type battleship could throw at least eight shells at a target at that range every minute. This arrangement would allow the captain to destroy his enemy at greater ranges, clearly a positive in naval warfare. Space once allotted to 6-inch and 8-inch secondary batteries was now considered wasteful. The multi-caliber

An Italian dreadnought, the pre-World War I *Andrea Doria*. This 24,000-ton ship mounted a main battery of 12-inch guns and a secondary battery of 6-inch weapons. There were to have been at least four more dreadnoughts laid down, yet the onset of war prevented further construction. In the 1930s, the *Andrea Doria* and other Italian prewar dreadnoughts were substantially rebuilt to prepare them for the next war. Modernization within limits was allowed under the Washington Naval Arms Limitation Treaty. The *Andrea Doria* was extended another 35.5 feet in length, and its horsepower was more than doubled to produce 85,000 shaft horsepower, with a speed topping 27 knots. The ship served for fifty years, until 1961. *Author's Collection*

secondary battery was of questionable value if it either reduced the barrels in the main battery or interfered with its operation.

A ship with its main battery of 12-inch guns solved problems of storage, training, and spare parts, as well as many technical and mechanical difficulties characteristic of multiple-gun types. Much of the vindication for the dreadnought concept and design was based on actual events that took place in the 1905 Battle of Tsushima. Japan's Admiral Togo defeated Russia's popular Admiral Rozhestvensky when his force sank twenty-two of thirty-seven ships in Rozhestvensky's force—60 percent of the Russian Navy that had been sent to destroy Togo. All eight Russian battleships were either sunk or surrendered to Togo, a humiliating defeat that has been rarely surpassed in naval warfare.

During the interwar years, the United States Navy thrilled its public by parading the battle fleet off the coast of Southern California. There was no greater sight that a dozen battleships steaming into Los Angeles Harbor with destroyers and cruisers. The power and might of these ships openly proved that the U.S. Navy was "second to none." The battleship in the bottom of the frame is one of the three *New Mexico*-class ships. The main battery of these ships ranged from 12-inch to 16-inch; however, without credible antiaircraft firepower, the ships were doomed. The reign of the all–big-gun dreadnought was brought to an end less than a quarter century after the HMS *Dreadnought* was launched. The aircraft carrier with its dive bombers and torpedo planes ensured this. *Author's Collection*

The Soviet navy battleship *Marat,* a 23,606-ton dreadnought that stole design features from Italy, Great Britain, and Japan. The lack of indigenous naval designers in Russia accounted for the poor quality of many of the country's warships before and during World War II. It was not until the latter half of the twentieth century that Soviet naval architecture showed real improvement. The *Marat,* which was funded in 1907 and received fifty-one design proposals from around the world, was actually created by the Italian naval architect Cuniberti. He had been the real moving force behind the dreadnought concept that Great Britain employed in 1906. The *Marat,* built in 1911, was a poor compromise, and was rebuilt at least twice during its nondescript career. It leaked, was rat- and insect-infested, and aside from being miserable to live aboard, had too little armor in crucial places and inadequate antiaircraft protection. In World War II it did assist in the defense of Leningrad as a floating artillery battery. The *Marat* was broken up in 1953. *Author's Collection*

There were two lessons burned into the souls of all far-thinking navalists: (1) a full broadside of heavy armament against an enemy at near-point-blank range had a devastating effect, and (2) the ever-popular and massive number of weapons in the secondary battery was of no real value. Their shell splashes merely interfered with those of the main battery, and a secondary battery of differing calibers merely deceived the gunners as to battle damage assessments. Knowing where your main-battery shells were hitting was absolutely vital to gunners attempting to find the range, and keep on target.

The dreadnought concept was not without enemies, because it was far different than what most senior serving officers were accustomed to. As their com-

mands became second rate overnight, naval officers saw the possibility of flag rank becoming elusive and strongly objected to the new battleships. But these shortsighted officers and politicians were fighting a losing battle. Britain's Admiral Fisher was a favorite of the conservative Queen Victoria, and as the first sea lord, he was able to sway Royal Navy strategy and future ship types. And his and Cuniberti's sweeping concept of an all-big-gun dreadnought with turbine power caught on internationally overnight.

As other navies rushed to design and build dreadnoughts, all previous battleships were consigned to the backwaters of naval importance. It was just a matter of time before the pre-dreadnoughts were scrapped to

The Italians ceded the battleship *Giulio Cesare* to Stalin's navy in March 1949 as reparations for war damages A dreadnought, the *Giulio Cesare* was designed in 1911 and rebuilt during the interwar period. After World War II, the Allies transferred the obsolete ship to the Soviets instead of more modern naval hardware. Renamed the *Novorossisk* (Z-11) by the Soviets, it was destroyed by an old German ground mine in October 1955. This served as a catalyst to rid the Soviet navy of its tired and outmoded officers and ships. It also put the Soviet navy on the path to becoming a blue-water naval superpower. *Author's Collection*

The German pocket battleship *Admiral Graf Spee* is accompanied into Montevideo Harbor by the Uruguayan patrol ship *Uruguay* on December 14, 1939. The *Graf Spee* was termed a *panzerschiff* (armored ship), raiding cruiser, commerce cruiser, or pocket battleship, depending on which diplomat was speaking. The 16,020-ton full load ship had fought an exciting battle with three British cruisers up the River Plate. Only one of the cruisers, HMNZS *Achilles*, was not seriously damaged. *Author's Collection.*

provide steel for the newer ships. With the end of World War I, full anchorages of obsolete ships awaited the scrap breakers' torch. The U.S. Navy was no different, and anchorages such as the Philadelphia Navy Yard were crowded with over a hundred thousand tons of outmoded, pre-dreadnought ships. It was the same in France, Great Britain, Italy, Japan, and other competitive navies around the world.

THE BATTLE CRUISER

In addition to the pre-dreadnought warships, Fisher sold the Royal Navy on the notion that "speed was armor." Consequently, a hybrid between the superbattleship and the heavily armed cruiser was developed as the battle cruiser. It was an idea that really sounded good on paper: a warship with battleship armament, speed in excess of 26 knots, and a sacrifice of armor to enable heavy weapons to be fitted. In Great Britain, the first of these was the HMS *Inflexible* in 1908. What a battle cruiser could not sink, it could avoid with its superior speed.

Based on the enthusiasm of the Royal Navy, the U.S. Navy as well as others considered the battle cruiser a very important addition to their fleets. As World War I wound down, the United States laid out plans for the six-ship *Constellation* class of battle cruiser. These ships were to displace 43,500 tons on a hull 874 feet in length, with a beam of 105 feet. They would be driven by turbo-electric propulsion plants generating 180,000 horsepower.

HMS *Hood*, a battle cruiser, was considered to be the most powerful and dependable warship in the Royal Navy. It displaced over 41,000 tons full load, and was capable of 31 knots on 144,000 shaft horsepower. Its main battery consisted of eight 15-inch guns in four turrets, yet it was deficient in armor protection compared to other ships displacing over 40,000 tons and mounting large weapons. Such was the design of the battle cruiser—fast but vulnerable. However, to the British public, the *Hood* represented Great Britain and the empire's power at sea, and for twenty years it was considered the finest warship in the world—a real icon of the sea. *U.S. Navy*

The crew of the *Hood* paints the hull and superstructure before the actual day that the great battle cruiser would eventually face its nemesis, the German battleship *Bismarck*. In mid-May 1941, the *Bismarck* and heavy cruiser *Prinz Eugen* were sighted by a reconnaissance Spitfire leaving a fiord in Norway. It was likely that they would break out into the Atlantic convoy routes and sink vitally needed shipping coming from America. The German ships met the *Hood* and consort HMS *Prince of Wales* on May 24, 1941, in the Denmark Strait. Salvoes from both German ships struck the *Hood* just aft of Stack No. 2, and the mighty ship exploded in a cataclysmic few seconds. Only three of the 1,420 crew survived. It was as if the ship had vaporized in an instant. The fallacy of matching a lightly armored battle cruiser against a true battleship was graphically portrayed. *Author's Collection*

Maximum speed was designed at 33.25 knots. The main battery had eight 16-inch 50-caliber guns in four turrets with two barrels each, and two turrets superfiring forward and aft. There would also be a secondary battery of sixteen 6-inch 53-caliber guns. The proposed *Constellation* class would have a 7-inch hull belt of armor, barbettes at 9 inches, the conning tower at 12 inches, and the main deck at 1.5 inches. Luckily for the U.S. Navy, these ships fell to the ax of international naval armaments limitations in 1922. Two were spared for conversion to heavy aircraft carriers: the USS *Lexington* (CV-2) and USS *Saratoga* (CV-3). Using battle cruiser hulls for these large aircraft carriers was a far more efficient use of steel and manpower. As World War II would soon reveal, the *Constellation* class battle cruisers could not have survived against any concentrated attack by modern battleships, submarines, and especially dive bombers. A 1.5-inch main-deck armor plate would have been disastrous to the battle cruiser.

Naval combat during World War I was hardly a real test of the new dreadnought or the fledgling concept of the battle cruiser. It did prove the viability of aircraft in naval warfare, and the submarine became a popular and necessary evil for a navy to succeed. The one massive clash between German and British naval forces took place at Jutland. Although the outcome was considered a victory by both belligerents, the losses told a different story. The Royal Navy lost three battle cruisers, three cruisers, and eight destroyers in addition to 6,067 officers and men. On the other hand, Germany lost one battleship, one battle cruiser, four cruisers, and five destroyers, plus 1,017 officers and ratings. The Royal Navy boasted of a strategic victory by keeping the Germans bottled up in port for the rest of the war. The Germans claimed a tactical victory by the numbers of ships destroyed and men killed. Based on this rather flimsy rationale, both did deserve to be designated as the victors.

One of the primary reasons for the heavy loss of British battle cruisers was that they were integrated into the battle line among the heavily armored battleships. Ships like the German *Lutzow* and British *Invincible*, *Indefatigable*, and *Queen Mary* were not made for battle-line combat. Simply because a warship displaced over 30,000 tons and mounted battleship-like weaponry did not ensure that it could withstand the punishment of opposing battleships. Speed was not allowed to be a factor in this type of combat, a fact that ultimately doomed the battle cruiser. Plunging fire from the opposing battle line easily dispatched these ships.

As to the dreadnought, which morphed into the battleship, serious alterations were still needed to make this ship type a realistic competitor in modern naval combat. Its adversaries were not simply other more powerful battleships; now there were submarines, aircraft, and destroyers with powerful and accurate armor-piercing torpedoes.

BATTLESHIP MODERNIZATION PROGRAMS
Many governments had invested vast fortunes in building dreadnoughts and battle cruisers before, during, and shortly after World War I. The Naval Arms Limitation Treaty signed in Washington, D.C., in 1922 provided for a ratio of capital ships based on a number of factors. The five major maritime powers—United Kingdom, United States, France, Italy, and Japan—were to be bound by certain ratios. For example, Great Britain was compelled to reduce its capital ship inventory from forty-four ships

The German battleship *Bismarck*. The *Bismarck* and sister *Tirpitz* became the reigning monarchs of the sea just after the loss of the indestructible *Hood*. The *Bismarck* was 823 feet in length with a beam of 118 feet, and she displaced 41,700 tons. (*Tirpitz* displaced 52,600 tons, yet was much the same as the *Bismarck* in all other dimensions.) The *Bismarck*'s main armament was eight 15-inch weapons in four turrets. The *Hood* met the *Bismarck* at 0537 hours, and opened fire at 0553 hours at distance of 14.5 miles. The German stereoscopic range finders were the finest in any navy, and the rounds from the *Bismarck* straddled the *Hood* immediately. Seven minutes after their first salvoes, the *Bismarck* and *Prinz Eugen* hit the *Hood* with armor-piercing shells which penetrated the almost unarmored decks. The end of the *Hood* came within a nanosecond, and fire was then shifted to the *Prince of Wales*. The mighty icon of the seas that ensured that Britannia ruled the waves was gone. *Author's Collection*

in 1918 to twenty ships. The United States followed suit; however, other signatories did not obey the letter and spirit of the treaty. There were objections to verification procedures, and Japan was insulted by being in the lowest-ratio category. Thus, the Japanese government was completely uncooperative.

As the years went by, nations began to rebuild and modernize existing battleships, yet also added few new ships. Great Britain's HMS *Queen Elizabeth* was launched in 1913, displaced 33,000 tons, boasted eight 15-inch guns in its main battery, and could achieve a speed of 24 knots from an oil-fired turbine engine. It went through two major reconstructions and soldiered

on to make major contributions during World War II. The same was true of many of the larger dreadnoughts launched before and during World War I in the American, Japanese, Italian, and French navies. Some of the most important changes were the conversion of power from coal to oil, and the addition of antiaircraft weaponry such as the 5-inch 25-caliber dual-purpose guns on the American battleships. Many of the other nations rebuilt battleship superstructures and added antiaircraft defenses in concert with anti-torpedo bulges to ward off serious damage from aerial- or submarine-launched torpedoes. Improved steering and command, control, and communication systems were

An artist's rendition of the *Bismarck* on the sea bed. After the sinking of the HMS *Hood*, Winston Churchill staked his political career on locating and sinking the *Bismarck*. It was a crusade to destroy that which had destroyed Britain's icon of the sea. The *Bismarck* was leaking forward from the engagement with the *Hood* and *Prince of Wales*, and from that time on, was hounded by every asset in the Royal Navy. Battleships and aircraft from carriers brought within extreme range hammered the running ship as it attempted to reach the French coast. If the *Bismarck* could have come within range of the Luftwaffe, roles would have been reversed, and the Royal Navy would have been on the run. On May 27, 1941, the *Bismarck* met its end at 1036 hours. It had been hit by aerial and destroyer-launched torpedoes and then by an unceasing pummeling by battleships HMS *King George V* and HMS *Rodney*. Churchill had his revenge on Hitler, and vindication for the British public. *U.S. Navy*

also added. The days of fighting a warship from an open quarterdeck had ended.

Despite all of the technological changes in naval warfare, including the presence of aircraft carriers, it was still the mighty battleship that a nation's people gauged their safety by. The bigger the ship and the greater the number of weapons, the more safe a people felt from belligerent neighbors that might have designs on conquering their country. As an example, the HMS *Hood*, completed in 1918, was in reality a paper tiger desperately in need of additional and strategically placed armor. The *Hood* was protected by only 1.5 to 2 inches of armor on its decks, and its other vital areas were likewise protected based on Admiral Jackie Fisher's "speed is armor" dictum. However, to the untrained eye, this magnificent warship signified protection and power in its 45,200 tons. Its opponents were not deceived, and when the opportunity arose, the *Hood* was destroyed in just a few minutes of concentrated fire.

A painting of the *Yamato* in all of its glory. This ship and sister *Musashi*, once unveiled to the world and the Japanese public, were icons of all-gun glory at sea. The third sister became the *Shinano*, a carrier. It was sunk, literally on its sea trials. The *Yamato* and the *Musashi* were lost in the last years of the war by massive attacks from carrier planes. In essence, none of this class, which consumed nearly a quarter of a million tons of steel and other resources, were of any value to the Japanese war effort. They may have given hope to a struggling public that was being bombed nightly by B-29s, but it was small compensation. *Author's Collection*

The older battleships and battle cruisers did not have propulsion plants that could be modified to squeeze out five or six extra knots. However, they were able to add a multitude of smaller weapons for close-in defense against attacking aircraft. Additionally, cruisers and destroyers could be employed to protect the battlewagons against submarines and other destroyers.

But these changes could not protect the ships from the faster and better-armed battleships that they would encounter in wars to come. In the early months of World War II, the German battleship *Bismarck*, which had two more decades of technological improvements to draw upon when it took to the water in the 1930s, sunk the aging HMS *Hood* with a few well-placed salvoes. Japanese naval

On the other side of the globe, Japanese shipyard workers hurry to complete the monster battleship, the Imperial Japanese Navy (IJN) *Yamato*. In 1937, the Japanese war machine began construction of the three-ship *Yamato* class of superbattleships. The Japanese Government defied the international accord on ship construction, and walked out of the 1936 conference in rebelliousness. The *Yamatos* would top 71,000 tons full load and mount the largest weapon to go to sea—the 18.1-inch gun. The class had three turrets with a total of nine 18.1 guns. The ships were 863 feet in length and also had twelve 6-inch guns as well as twelve 5-inch guns. Its secondary battery was the equivalent of two small light cruisers and two large-size destroyers combined! This class also carried a seven-plane air group with catapults aft as well as hangers. *U.S. Navy*

aircraft sunk another battle cruiser, the HMS *Repulse,* on December 10, 1941, within ninety minutes of sighting it.

THE DEATH OF INTERNATIONAL COOPERATION

The nations of the Naval Arms Limitation Treaty of 1922 gathered to update the treaty in 1927, 1930, 1932, 1934, and 1936. But by the last meeting, the spirit of cooperation, albeit hypocritical, was dead. In 1936, the Japanese delegation walked out of the proceedings and refused to abide by the tenets of this or any treaty that stopped the Imperial Navy from taking its place in the sun. The Japanese plans to build the massive *Yamato*-class battleships (see chapter 1) had already been confirmed beyond the rumor stage. These plans were a clear violation of the treaty and the primary reason for Japan abandoning the 1936 meeting.

In actuality, most of the nations had secretly violated the terms. The original Washington "Cherry Tree" Treaty signed in 1922 had all of the best motives, yet expecting to

Four of Japan's warships moored together and representing the best that the nations had to offer in naval battles. From front to rear are the: *Nagato* at 39,130 tons full load. This ship was commissioned in November 1920 and escaped the Washington Naval Treaty cuts. It mounted eight 16-inch 45-caliber guns in four turrets. It was sunk in Operation Crossroads, the atomic weapon test at Bikini Atoll, on July 29, 1946. *Kirishima* (battlecruiser) 26,230 tons full load. This battlecruiser was commissioned in April 1915 and mounted eight 14-inch 45-caliber guns. It was sunk by the USS *South Dakota* and the USS *Washington* on November 15, 1942. The *Kirishima* held its own against the *South Dakota* before the *Washington* appeared. *Ise* at 36,000 tons full load. It was commissioned in December 1917, and mounted twelve 14-inch 45-caliber guns. This ship was lost on July 28, 1945, due to massive carrier air attacks. *Hiei* at 26,000 tons full load. Its main battery consisted of eight 14-inch 45-caliber guns. It entered active service in August 1914, and was sunk by cruisers and aircraft on November 13, 1942.

In this mid-1930s image, the USS *Arizona* (BB-39) which was a sister to the USS *Pennsylvania* (BB-38) steams along at a moderate speed, yet the oil smoke problem has yet to be solved, as evidenced by the mainmast. The *Arizona* and *Pennsylvania* were the first battleships to employ the turbine, and could make 21 knots with ease. Both 37,624-ton full load ships were armed with twelve 14-inch 45-caliber guns, yet the antiaircraft weaponry was wholly inadequate. The *Arizona* was lost within minutes of the beginning of the attack on Pearl Harbor when a bomb exploded in its forward magazine. Since that explosion on December 7, 1941, the ship has never moved and is still a commissioned vessel albeit a gravesite for 1,177 officers and men. The *Arizona* is the ultimate battleship icon of the twentieth century. *U.S. Navy*

The USS *Alabama* (BB-60) was one of the ships that led to the development of the final American battleships—the *Iowa*s. It carried nine 16-inch guns, and almost every spare location on deck was covered with small antiaircraft weapons. This was to be the new type of battleship—one capable of bombarding shore targets, fighting it out with enemy warships, and protecting the fast carriers with a barrage of antiaircraft fire. This ship is currently in memorial status in Mobile, Alabama. *Author's Collection*

rein in nations for over fifteen years was naïve. By 1936, the treaty was no longer viable and hamstrung participants' international ambitions. And so one nation after another began to be secretive and lie about their intentions. All nations were building larger, more potent warships and planning the war that politicians, diplomats, and military officers were certain was soon to come. It was no longer "if," but "when" would the war begin.

Germany, which was by then ruled by the thugs of the Nazi party, openly defied the Versailles Treaty, and all but dared the European powers and the United States to do something about its outrageous international conduct. The German navy termed its three new 16,000-ton pocket battleships, which mounted six 11-inch guns, "commerce cruisers" or heavy cruisers or even armored battle cruisers—anything but battleships. In reality, the three heavily armed *Panzerschiffs* (armored ships)—the *Admiral Von Graf Spee*, *Lutzow*, and *Admiral Scheer*—were battleships in cruiser clothing. They were based on a World War I battle-cruiser design (*Mackensen*) that was considered to be the best concept of its day. It was still able to hold its own twenty years later. Germany also began construction of a surface fleet, including heavy battleships of 54,000 tons, such as the *Tirpitz* and *Bismarck*. The other powers did nothing to stop Germany, except send notes of protest through diplomatic channels.

Meanwhile, the Japanese had more aircraft carriers in the Pacific than the United States did. Their battleships

Great Britain's last battleship, the HMS *Vanguard*, was built toward the end of World War II and lasted only a few years before being broken up. The British public could no longer afford the luxury of even one battleship. Although the battleship represented national power, Great Britain now sought respect through other means. *Author's Collection*

and cruisers were highly modernized and mounted the 24-inch Long Lance torpedo, which would be one of the deadliest weapons in the early stages of the naval war in the Pacific.

Most of the future belligerents had modernized their older ships to the maximum extent possible by the mid-1930s. Thus, the United States Navy's fifteen battleships were more capable, but still the most modern was

the *West Virginia* class built in 1923. Eighteen years later, the U.S. Navy commissioned its next battleship, the 44,800-ton (fully loaded) USS *North Carolina* (BB-55) and its sister, the USS *Washington* (BB-56). They were followed by the four-ship *South Dakota* class, and both classes underscored the next and final American battleship, the *Iowa* class.

THE FATE OF THE SUPERBATTLESHIPS

The Japanese 70,000-ton superbattleships *Yamato* and *Musashi* met their end at sea, as did the rest of the battleships in the Imperial Japanese Navy. The *Yamato* and *Musashi*, thought to be unsinkable, used what fuel remained in Japanese stockpiles to disrupt Allied landings in the Southern Philippines in October 1944. The plan was for them to first sink the landing force; barring that, they were to ram the ships into the landing zone and with their huge main battery destroy the Allied attack. In hindsight, this was a fool's errand. The *Musashi* absorbed twenty-six aerial torpedoes and thirty 500- to 1,000-pound bomb hits before it succumbed. The *Yamato* had never fired its guns in anger until it came upon U.S. Admiral Clifton Sprague's escort group of jeep carriers, destroyers, and destroyer escorts. The Battle of Samar played out like David versus Goliath, with David remaining on the field.

In early April 1945, the *Yamato* was subjected to a pair of American naval air strikes. The first consisted of

The USS *Massachusetts* (BB-59) in Battleship Cove, Massachusetts. This *South Dakota*-class battleship has been a memorial since June 4, 1965. The 45,000-ton full load battleship had three sisters (*South Dakota, Indiana,* and *Alabama*), and all mounted a main battery of nine 16-inch 45-caliber guns. With the *North Carolina* class, these ships led the way to the ultimate battleship—the *Iowa* class. *Author's Collection*

The USS *North Carolina* (BB-55), sister to the USS *Washington* and precursor to the *Iowa* and *South Dakota* classes. The *North Carolina* is currently a memorial ship in Wilmington, North Carolina. This class was the first built after the USS *West Virginia*, which was constructed in 1923. There had been a long hiatus between ships, and the *North Carolina* was the first fast battleship built by the U.S. Navy. Other nations had long surpassed the American navy with a variety of modern battleship classes by the time that the *North Carolina* was commissioned on April 9, 1941. *Author's Collection*

280 aircraft, the second of 100 carrier-launched bombers and torpedo planes. The *Yamato* absorbed twelve torpedoes and five heavy-iron bomb hits. Suddenly a tremendous explosion broke the battleship's back, and she slid under sea, taking 2,498 officers and men to their deaths. Daring and resolute pilots had sunk these icons of the Japanese navy with some of the U.S. Navy's flimsiest aircraft and most inexpensive weapons.

The German giants, the *Bismarck* and *Tirpitz*, were also destroyed in World War II, as were the ships in the German capital fleet.

A few French heavy ships survived the war. The Italian battleships, dubbed the "cardboard warships" by their own crews, sacrificed too much armor for speed and were easily sunk. A few of the Italian warships were ceded to the Soviet Union.

As to the Royal Navy, maintaining a large battle fleet was out of the question. The Royal Treasury could not support battleships. One final offering, the 44,500-ton, 814-foot-long HMS *Vanguard*, was launched in 1944, but was nearly obsolete by the time it was introduced to the fleet. Its main battery consisted of eight 15-inch guns and its top speed was 29 knots—not a significant improvement on previous classes. Despite its popularity with the British royal family as a backup yacht, the *Vanguard* was placed in reserve in 1956, then broken up in 1960. In some respects, Great Britain's last battleship went from the builder's yard to the ship

breakers at Faslane Naval Base without achieving any worthy military purpose.

The Soviet navy, as well as other European navies, maintained their battleships until the late 1950s and early 1960s. Beyond that period, there was no point to saddling a nation's people with the cost of a weapon of dubious value.

The United States scrapped all but a very few of its most modern battleships. By 1959, the USS *Maryland, Colorado, West Virginia, California,* and *Tennessee,* along with dozens of World War II–era cruisers, destroyers, and other superfluous craft, had been towed from various reserve fleets to the scrap yards around the nation. In 1960, there were no active battleships in the U.S. Navy; however, there were ten held in reserve: two of the *North Carolina* class, four of the *South Dakota* class, and, the most powerful, the four of the *Iowa* class. By 1965, all but the *Iowa* class were removed from the Naval Vessel Register. The USS *Massachusetts, Alabama,* and *North Carolina* were preserved in permanent battleship memorials, and the others were sent to the ship breakers, leaving the *Iowa* class in reserve. No politician or senior naval officer had the heart to dispose of these magnificent warships, which could possibly be utilized in the future.

For the USS *New Jersey*, it was merely a few years before she was called upon to destroy North Vietnamese targets in support of ground troops ashore. The *New*

The USS *New Jersey* (BB-62) after being refurbished for the Vietnam War. Its 16-inch guns were necessary to pound North Vietnamese targets close to the shore and the communication and supply systems between the north and south. The experiment did not extend to the other three *Iowa*-class battleships, and within a year, the *New Jersey* was back in mothballs. *Author's Collection*

Jersey's tour duty off Vietnam lasted from September 30, 1968, until April 3, 1969. The battlewagon remained on station for 120 days pounding enemy targets into rubble with 1,900-pound shells. Surprisingly, its analog computers were sufficient for the task and would again be used in the mid-1980s.

Each nation that possessed a battleship in its navy considered itself one of the superpowers of the twentieth century. Even certain cash-strapped South American nations with old dreadnoughts were accorded great respect by neighboring countries. A fleet with a battleship

The ultimate icon of the twentieth-century battleship—the USS *Arizona* (BB-39), is now on the bottom of Pearl Harbor and a national memorial of the American navy and the people of the United States. A survivor of the attack on December 7th, 1941, Everett Hyland ponders while standing on the memorial, which spans the beam of the battleship. In the background lies the USS *Missouri* (BB-63), or the *"Mighty Mo."* It was on the *Missouri*, an *Iowa*-class battleship, that the surrender document was signed that ended the most terrible war in the history of mankind. The *Arizona* signifies the beginning of that war, at least for the United States. Everett was serving aboard the *Arizona*'s sister, the USS *Pennsylvania*, which was in dry dock a few hundred yards away. The *Arizona* had thirty-three sets of brothers, twenty-nine twins, and four sets of triplets in its crew on that morning that changed history forever. *U.S. Navy*

was superior and brought fear to those who challenged their power. Nations without battleships took great pains to defeat these ships with torpedoes, massive explosives, armor-piercing bombs, mines, torpedoes, and every weapon conceivable.

After the heyday of the battleships, the United States had the greatest number and today still possesses several in memorial status, including the USS *Iowa* (BB-61), which is eventually to be a museum ship somewhere on the American western coastline. These ships will always inspire awe, respect, and a feeling of protection against potential enemies. They are truly icons of naval hardware and of the twentieth century.

An aft photograph of the *North Carolina* after it was launched, yet before being completely fitted out. The antiaircraft batteries have yet to be brought aboard. Initially they consisted of 1.1-inch guns and .50-caliber water-cooled machine guns. Neither weapon was actually of any real value, because for aiming they depended on the human optical factor, and that was not quick enough to track and destroy modern fast aircraft. *U.S. Navy*

CHAPTER THREE

BUILDING THE
IOWA CLASS

The *Iowa* class was not planned to be the final type of battleship to be built by the United States Navy. As the *Iowa* class was being approved and the keel being laid on the lead ship, the USS *Iowa*, bigger and more powerful battleships were being considered. This rationale was rampant despite the victories by aircraft and submarines in all of the theaters of World War II. In fact, the drawing board was already weighted down with blueprints of the four turret (twelve 16 inch 50 caliber guns) *Montana* class, the five-ship follow-on class to the six-ship *Iowa* class. Each *Montana* would displace 70,965 tons full load and have a secondary battery of twenty radar-directed 5-inch 54-caliber guns. There was even some talk of an even larger battleship, but the war ended and fortunately, so did many dreams and schemes. As it happened, the *Iowa* class was the last series of American battleships built, and they are the finest of this class ever to sail for any navy.

In essence, the design of the *Iowa* was founded on the main weapon to be used, the 16-inch gun. There was some talk of mounting 18-inch 47-caliber guns in the main battery, but the modern 16-inch weapon was far superior. Their use also saved money. During the international battleship race immediately following World War I, a substantial number of 16-inch gun barrels were forged. The building competition was halted by the 1922 Naval Arms Limitation Treaty, and several partially built American battleships were broken up on the building ways or sunk as targets, thus leaving a surplus of the barrels. Six battleships of the *South Dakota* class, authorized in 1917, had reached the 30 percent or more completion phase, and yielded seventy-two 16-inch 50-caliber barrels.

The 16-inch gun has proven to be reliable and well suited to the hull and overall strength of the frames. The 18-inch gun would have been too much weapon for what amounted to a 45,000-ton ship. When the 16-inch 50-caliber guns were fired in salvo, the *Iowa*-class ships held together, whereas the 18-inch guns would have shaken the ships apart. A 16-inch salvo is loud, but does not move the ship to port or starboard in the water.

Another consideration for the design of the *Iowa* was the international political situation. The United States subscribed to the 1922 International Naval Arms

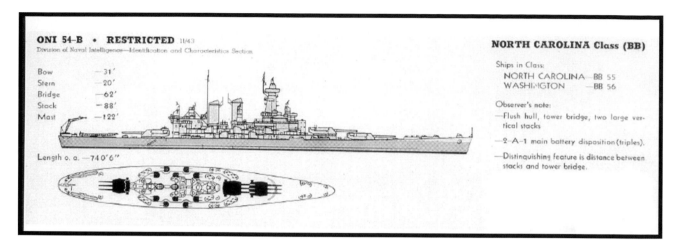

A line drawing of the USS *North Carolina* (BB-55). This design is reminiscent of certain capital ships in various European navies. The forward conning tower is pronounced, the stacks are rather high, and there is a great distance between them. *U.S. Navy*

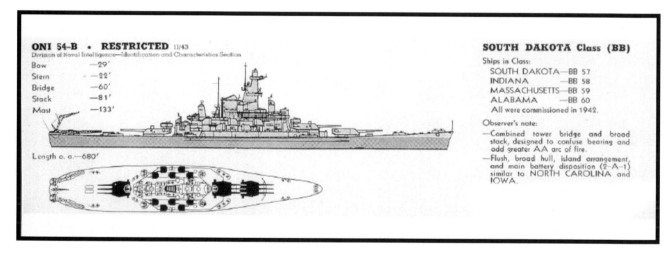

A line drawing of the USS *South Dakota* (BB-57). In reality, the *South Dakota* did not have two of the 5-inch mounts as shown. The *South Dakota* had eighteen 5-inch 38-caliber guns. The forward mounts had 40mm quad antiaircraft weapons instead. In one battle after another, this ship acquitted itself well. It shot down twenty-six enemy aircraft in one battle, and was known as "Battleship X" or the "Big Bastard." *U.S. Navy*

Limitation Treaty, but by 1936, most nations, including the United States, had begun planning for the time when there would be no treaty. The U.S. Navy planning staff was anxious to begin construction on some new ideas of its own.

Before the *Iowa* class would be introduced, the *North Carolina* class and the *South Dakota* class had to make their debuts. These were the first of the "fast" battleships in the U.S. Navy and set the stage for the six ships in the *Iowa* class.

THE *NORTH CAROLINA* AND *SOUTH DAKOTA* CLASSES

The *North Carolina* class included its namesake ship (BB-55) and her sister, the USS *Washington* (BB-56); both were authorized between 1934 and 1936. Under the auspices of the 1922 treaty provisions, they were to replace the almost ancient USS *New York* (1914) and USS *Arkansas* (1912).

Although the *North Carolina* class was restricted to 35,000 tons, it ultimately displaced 44,800 tons in the

The USS *Alabama* (BB-60) in 1945 after serving in the Atlantic and almost every theater in the Pacific. The ships in the *South Dakota* class had some deficiencies, but in general held together well, and often were in the thick of sea battles–battles that never will be fought again. The *Alabama* is on display in Mobile, Alabama, as a battleship memorial. *Author's Collection*

second year of World War II. The *North Carolina* class also set the stage for the triple-barrel 16-inch 50-caliber gun, and its shaft horsepower of 121,000 enabled a speed of 27 knots. This speed was higher than that of contemporary American battleships, but less than that of ships of other nations.

The major disadvantage of this class was the extremely poor habitability for the crew. The machinery was rearranged in the hull, and there were few portholes to allow proper ventilation. This arrangement was nearly unbearable in the tropics, as there was no free flow of air through the ship.

The next battleship class was the four-ship *South Dakota*. These were designed to replace the USS *Nevada* (1916), USS *Oklahoma* (1916), USS *Pennsylvania* (1916), and USS *Texas*

(1914). This class initially displaced 35,000 tons, and this displacement was increased to 45,200 during World War II.

The *South Dakota* class also mounted nine 16-inch 50-caliber guns in three triple-barrel turrets. There were two turrets forward—the number two turret superfired over number one—and a single turret aft. The shaft

The *South Dakota* takes a big wave over the bow. Note the amount of seawater flooding the area between the bow and Turrent No. 1. *U.S. Navy*

The USS *South Dakota* fights off Japanese carrier aircraft during the Battle of Santa Cruz Islands on October 26, 1942. The battleship and the carrier USS *Enterprise* had been rearmed with 40mm Bofors guns recently, and they ripped the Japanese attackers to pieces. The *South Dakota* was credited with shooting down twenty-six attackers in less than three hours and saving what was by that time the last U.S. aircraft carrier remaining in the Pacific. *U.S. Navy*

horsepower had been increased to 130,000, which was 9,000 more than the *North Carolina* class had. The big difference between the *South Dakota* and the *North Carolina* was the dimensions. The *South Dakota*'s machinery was rearranged to the point where it could fit everything necessary in a hull 680 feet long and 108 feet 2 inches extreme width. This rearrangement saved a great deal of weight, thus allowing more armor protection over critical areas. In the slugging match that the *South Dakota* would eventually find itself in with Japanese battleships, the armor was a life saver. In the Battle of Guadalcanal, the *South Dakota* absorbed forty-two hits, which did horrendous

damage, yet it was the Japanese battleship *Kirishima* that was sunk.

The *North Carolina* class had a length of 729 feet and a beam of 108 feet 1 inch. The difference between this class and the *South Dakota* was 49 feet for essentially the same package. The overall shortened dimension (length-to-beam ratio) of the *South Dakota* class reduced maneuverability and made the ship difficult to steer and respond. The *South Dakota* class also had one funnel as opposed the *North Carolina*'s two stacks.

THE *IOWA* CLASS

The planners that were designing the Iowa watched the

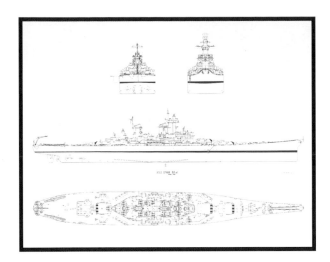

A line drawing of the USS *Iowa*. As can be seen, every vacant space on deck is crowded with Bofors quad 40mm antiaircraft guns and 20mm Oerlikon single-barrel close-in weapons. Much of the accuracy was dependent on the eyesight and depth perception of the individual gunner. *U.S. Navy*

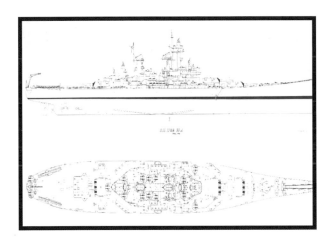

Another line drawing of the *Iowa* which, although somewhat distorted, provides a close view of the tremendous short-range firepower needed to keep enemy aircraft away from the ship and those she has been chosen to protect. *U.S. Navy*

progress on the *North Carolina* and *South Dakota* classes. They noted the deficiencies, which required correction if the navy was to have a true fast battleship. The new *Essex*-class carriers were easily capable of speeds over 30 knots, as were all of the destroyers and cruisers, and the battleship had to keep up. In doctrinal planning,

An *Iowa*-class battleship takes shape on the building ways as the internal machinery is fitted, and even some of the forward steel decking has been laid prior to the Burmese teak wooden overlay. *U.S. Navy*

the battleship had by default taken on two new combat roles in the Pacific. First, they were to escort the fast carriers by acting as a protector against aircraft. Second, they were called up to devastate enemy-held beachheads so that a landing force would not encounter too much difficulty. Overall, this meant that the *Iowa* class had to be able to maneuver with a fast-moving task force and have sufficient antiaircraft weapons to protect themselves and the aircraft carriers. In addition, the *Iowa* class had to mount at least nine 16-inch 50-caliber guns for shore bombardment.

The designers learned well from the efforts of those building the *South Dakota* and the *North Carolina* classes. The *Iowa* class copied the main and secondary armament type and location. However, it was over 200 feet longer than the *South Dakota* class. The machinery was more powerful, and the shaft horsepower was increased to 212,000. The increased horsepower enabled speeds in excess of 33 knots, and the hull extension beyond Turret

The enclosed bridge of an *Iowa*-class battleship that surrounds the armored conning tower. Under normal steaming conditions, the ship's command structure remained out on this open bridge area. When there were incoming missiles or shells, the party moved to the interior of the conning tower, where the armor would protect them from everything except multiple direct hits. *Author's Collection*

The outer bridge of the *Iowa*-class battleship USS *Missouri,* moored at Ford Island, Pearl Harbor. Ford Island is in the background, and the *Missouri* is moored aft of the USS *Arizona.* The outer bridge has many of the control and communication systems normally available on the inner bridge and in the armored citadel. *Author's Collection*

No. 1 was substantially greater than on previous battleships. The armor was increased and arrayed in such a way that it was integrated within the hull. The sides of this class of battleship were flush and rock solid.

A year before the keel of the *Iowa* was laid, it was proposed that a new main battery shell replace the 2,240-pound armor-piercing (AP) shell. This was done. The new 2,700-pound shell had a low initial velocity, yet its velocity had greater endurance.

The first two *Iowa*-class ships were the USS *Iowa* and the USS *New Jersey.* The next ships resulted in some strenuous argument with the Department of the Navy. A strong vocal faction wanted BB-63 and BB-64 to be slower battleships with twelve 16-inch 50-caliber guns. This preference was found to be absurd, as the only gain was a fourth turret, and 27-knot battleships were no longer considered to be the requisite fast battleship. A 33-knot ship was the minimum acceptable, and the plans, designs, and experiences of the *Iowa* and *New Jersey* fully justified the necessity of speed. The USS *Missouri* (BB-63) and USS *Wisconsin* (BB-64) won out as *Iowa*-class

A mid-war view of the USS *Iowa* and the camouflage paint scheme it was wearing. The paint schemes on battleships and, for that matter, most ships were always being changed to help fool the enemy. *U.S. Navy*

The crew's barbershop aboard an *Iowa*-class ship was just like any stateside barbershop, and hundreds of trims and haircuts were given weekly. At one time, sailors and officers were permitted to look like shaggy dogs, but a new chief of naval operations ended that practice. Ship's personnel were to be clean shaven and have appropriate haircuts. *Author's Collection*

The *Iowa*'s central passageway, known as "Broadway," extends from the forward conning tower aft to Turret No. 3. Off the passageway are vital access points to the lower decks, machine shops, and other areas important to the operations of the ship. Anyone who claims to have served aboard an *Iowa*-class battleship and has never heard of this passageway is fibbing, as it is the most famous of all passageways aboard this class of ship. *Author's Collection*

The ship's officers' laundry, where uniforms are cleaned and pressed. Having this readily available leaves no excuse for a leader to look rumpled in his uniform. *Author's Collection*

The captain's suite and where he sleeps. To the right and out of sight is a dining area for sixteen guests. This was used for officers and visiting dignitaries. *Author's Collection*

battleships, as did the USS *Illinois* (BB-65) and USS *Kentucky* (BB-66). These last two ships were only partially completed at the end of World War II, and thus were never completed.

The *Iowa* class was not only aesthetically beautiful, it was also the largest and most powerful battleship ever produced for the U.S. Navy. It cost $100 million during the early 1940s, and eventually topped 58,000 tons full-load displacement. It was the ultimate battleship design and was based on all of those that had gone before it. The entire class still exists, and that is a real tribute to any warship.

Crew's bunks with lock boxes for valuables. The crew also had lockers for their clothing and other items. The crew's accommodations were somewhat different than those of the captain: a good incentive for aspiring to higher rank! *Author's Collection*

Crew's cafeteria aboard an *Iowa*-class battleship. It operated just like any other cafeteria and was far more efficient than the old ways of institutional feeding of nearly two thousand men and women. *Author's Collection*

Aft aboard the USS *Iowa,* and the Mark 37 director for the secondary battery of 5-inch 38-caliber weapons. The Mark 37 is to the far right of the image, with a Mark 25 radar antenna on top of the director. To the center is the Mark 38 director for the main battery or aft 16-inch 50-caliber guns. They have been painted; however, painting ceased when Representative Richard Pombo ceded the vessel to the Port of Stockton against naval regulations. *Author's Collection*

The ship's bell (clearly requiring some polishing), up forward beneath a radio tower. *Author's Collection*

The USS *Iowa* (BB-61) looking aft from the bow. The barrels of Turrets No. 1 and 2 have covers over the openings. Turret two is now frozen in position and has never been repaired since the flareback of 1989. A plaque has been bolted on the bulkhead of the turret's interior paying tribute to those forty-seven who died during the flareback. As of mid-2006, only an occasional worker or writer-photographer (such as the authors) visit the ship. *Author's Collection*

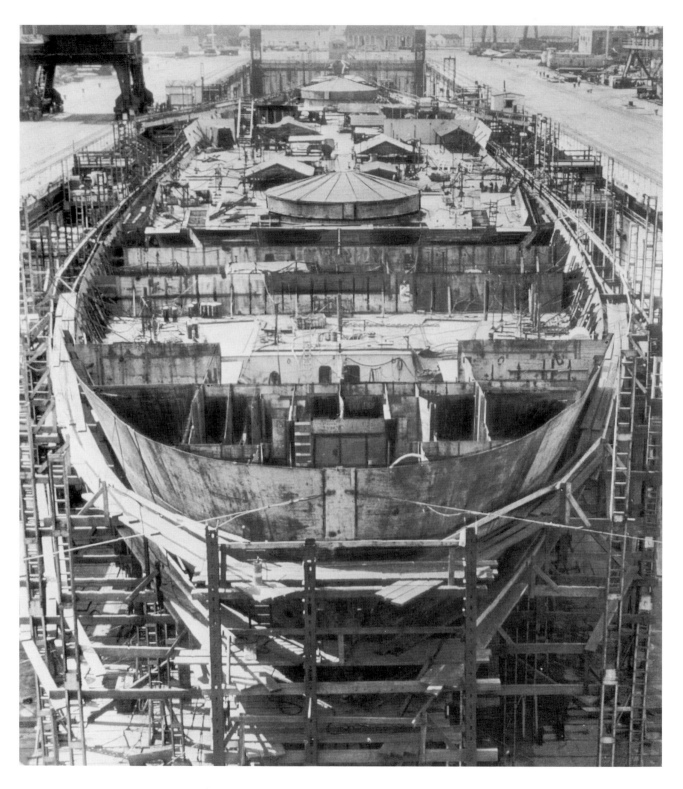

The unfinished hull of the USS *Kentucky* on September 20, 1947. This *Iowa*-class battleship was to have become a missile ship. This came to naught, and the ship actually provided parts for the other four completed *Iowa*-class battleships. On October 31, 1958, the *Kentucky* was scrapped. *Author's Collection*

The USS *Sacramento* (OE-1) moored in San Diego, California. One of the engines from the *Kentucky* was employed aboard this huge supply ship, and now the *Sacramento* has been decommissioned and will likely be scrapped in the near future. *Author's Collection*

Workers at the New York Navy Yard hurry to complete the lead ship of the *Iowa*-class battleship, the USS *Iowa* (BB-61). The Mark VII gun barrels have been installed in the No. 2 turret forward. The turret will house three 16-inch 50-caliber guns, and now requires its armored plating. *U.S. Navy*

Hundreds of visitors and high naval brass attend the commissioning of the new battleship, USS *Iowa* (BB-61) on February 22, 1943. The New York Navy Yard, like so many around the United States, worked twenty-four hours a day to build all types of ships, yet a battleship was a rarity, and the workers are proud of the job they have done. They never dreamed that the *Iowa* would still be part of the navy sixty-three years later. *U.S. Navy*

CHAPTER FOUR

USS *IOWA* IN WORLD WAR II

Construction on the battleship *Iowa* began at the New York Navy Yard on June 27, 1940, which was approximately seventeen months before the Japanese attacked Pearl Harbor. Before the United States entered into World War II, the New York Navy Yard was overwhelmed with workers and partially built ships. Everyone seemed to know that war was imminent for the United States, and the navy would play a crucial role.

The *Iowa* was a brand-new concept in battleship construction. It was not a dreadnought like its predecessors of World War I; it was a modern, heavily armed, and even more heavily armored warship that was built to absorb a great deal of punishment. It also could deal out a phenomenal amount of punishment in the form of nine 16-inch 50-caliber guns. These guns could fire an armor-piercing round weighing over a ton some 41,600 yards with a high degree of accuracy. With nine of these shells coming toward it, the target would almost certainly be destroyed or at least heavily damaged.

On August 27, 1942, just three weeks after the initial landings at Guadalcanal, the *Iowa* slid down the ways and into the water. Fitting-out took an additional six months,

and on February 22, 1943, this powerful, 887-foot-long, 57,600-ton full load battleship was commissioned. The ship had cost the American taxpayers $100 million. Its power plant could develop 212,000 shaft horsepower and would drive this huge ship at speeds of up to 33 knots, guaranteeing its ability to escort the fast carriers.

Two days after the commissioning ceremony was over, and with a complete crew, the *Iowa* sailed for Chesapeake Bay for a brief initial shakedown cruise. For the next few months, the new battleship extended its shakedown as it steamed up and down the Atlantic coast. Every piece of machinery and all of the weapons were thoroughly tested.

The *Iowa*'s career beginning was not all pleasant and without incident. On July 16, 1943, when the ship entered Casco Bay, Maine, from New York, the narrow channel's water was quite shallow. The *Iowa* passed over what might have been the wreck of an old freighter and sustained a 232-foot-long gash in its hull. The *Iowa*'s next port of call was the Boston Navy Yard and dry dock for immediate repair. The period in dry dock revealed that eighteen shell plates had to be replaced and that sixteen fuel tanks had been ruptured. Captain John L. McCrea was not found

The huge bow of the *Iowa* dominates this image, and has yet to be converted to accommodate the two 20mm Oerlikon close-in weapons. The ship is about to be launched. The chains hanging on each side of the bow will slow the ship as it slides into the water. Tons of grease and tallow are put on the ways to ensure that the new battleship slides easily, and divers check the water behind the *Iowa* to make certain that there are no obstructions. *U.S. Navy*

guilty of any negligence. The channel entrance to Casco Bay was reputed to be a ship killer, and other large warships had also touched bottom. (McCrea had been the former aide to President Franklin D. Roosevelt, who personally reviewed the incident.)

With repairs made and workmanship corrected in the yard during the rush to put the *Iowa* into the fleet, the battleship received orders to steam for Argentina and Newfoundland and to intercept and destroy the German surface raider *Tirpitz*. It was an interesting first assignment for a new battleship with a novice crew of 2,700 officers and enlisted ratings. However, the ship's weaponry and solid armor, up to 18 inches in certain locations, instilled great confidence in the men.

The *Tirpitz* was Germany's last surface threat of any real degree and had spent much of its career lurking in Norwegian fiords. There, this battleship, with its eight radar-directed 15-inch guns, tied up major elements of the British Royal Navy. This ship could not be allowed to destroy or interrupt the convoys being sent to the Russian port of Murmansk and other crucial areas in the north. Already, convoys had to deal with U-boat wolf packs and air attacks when they came within range of Nazi airfields in the Baltic area. The 52,600-ton full load, 823-foot-long *Tirpitz* was commissioned on February 22, 1941, just a few months before its infamous sister, the *Bismarck,* sank the HMS *Hood* and in turn was brought to bay by almost every asset in the Royal Navy. (The story of the *Bismarck* is one of the most discussed in World War II naval history. In the end, it was the battleships HMS *King George V* and HMS *Rodney* that settled the issue, and the *Bismarck* disappeared beneath the waves on May 27, 1941.)

The cover of *Life* magazine on October 30, 1944. The *Iowa* was featured in this issue, and enabled millions of Americans to see what their hard-earned war bonds were buying and what shipyards and the navy were achieving. *Author's Collection*

A U.S. Navy photo of their newest battleship—the USS *Iowa*. The *Iowa* mounted nine 16-inch guns in its main battery, twenty 5-inch 38-caliber dual-purpose guns in the ten turrets of the secondary battery for antiaircraft or surface threats, and eighty 40mm and 20mm guns for close-in defense. The *Iowa* class was formidable against air threats and shipping. Its first major assignment after launching was to move to the North Atlantic and take on the German sister to the now sunk *Bismarck*— the *Tirpitz*. The duel never happened. *U.S. Navy*

The *Tirpitz* was reportedly operating in Norwegian waters and not riding at anchor. The most powerful asset in the Atlantic that could neutralize this battleship was the brand-new *Iowa*. On August 27, 1943, the *Iowa* moved toward Newfoundland to destroy the *Tirpitz* if the German ship chose to move in that direction. The *Iowa* crew was confident in the outcome: another German battleship to the bottom of the Atlantic.

Unfortunately, this clash between titans was not to be. The *Iowa* spent several weeks awaiting the showdown, but the *Tirpitz* remained close to the protection of the Norwegian mountains and fiords. The *Tirpitz* did sortie for a raid on Spitzbergen, Norway, in Operation Silizien in September 1943. However, Adolf Hitler did not consider the Kriegsmarine battleship of any value, and ultimately, after several air attacks, the Royal Air Force sunk the ship on November 12, 1944. Lancaster bombers dropping 5-ton "tallboys" hit the ship with three of these mega bombs. The ship's armor

was pierced, and a magazine exploded and literally blew the ship to pieces. It then capsized and took a thousand sailors to their death.

The *Iowa* continued with its operations in the Atlantic and prepared to go to the Pacific theater of operations. First, however, the ship would play host to President Roosevelt and major military staff in a joint meeting with the leader of Russia, Joseph Stalin, and the prime minister of Great Britain, Winston Churchill. The meeting was to take place in Teheran, Iran, and was one of the most significant conferences of the nations that became known as the Big Three.

President Roosevelt required certain bathing and living conditions, as he had suffered infantile paralysis (polio), which had rendered him unable to walk or even stand. A large, square porcelain bathtub with stainless-steel railings was built in the quarters normally reserved for a fleet commander or battleship division commander. It was and is the only bathtub aboard any warship in the

United States Navy. (Prior to World War II, the president often used the heavy cruiser USS *Houston* (CA-30) for fishing trips and visits to Central and South American ports, yet its appointments were not on the scale of those aboard the *Iowa*.)

It was certain that the *Iowa* would be safe for the journey, and other ships were selected as escort craft. One of these ships was the USS *William D. Porter* (DD-579), a new *Fletcher*-class destroyer.

THE SAGA OF THE *IOWA* AND THE "WILLIE DEE"

From November 1943 until her bizarre loss in June 1945, the USS *William D. Porter* often met with various clever greetings whenever she entered port or joined naval ships. Until 1958, the incident that spawned the expressions,

"Don't shoot, we're Republicans!" or "What happened to the fish that got away?" was almost a cult secret of the United States Navy. The navy kept a lid on this incident until it was discovered by a *Miami News* reporter covering the destroyer crew's annual reunion in 1958. The Pentagon reluctantly confirmed the story, yet to this day, little official comment has been made by the Department of the Navy, which would prefer not to discuss it.

You see, the "*Willie Dee*," as the *Porter* was nicknamed, accidentally fired a live torpedo at the battleship USS *Iowa* on November 14, 1943, during a practice exercise. If this weren't bad enough, the *Iowa* was carrying President Franklin D. Roosevelt, Secretary of State Cordell Hull, and all of the country's World War II military brass to the Big Three conference in Tehran. Had the *Porter*'s torpedo struck the *Iowa* at the aiming point,

The German battleship *Tirpitz* running trials in 1941. In 1943, it was the major surface threat to shipping in the North Atlantic. The *Tirpitz* was actually designed at about the same time that the *Iowa* class was put on the drawing board, in the early-to-mid-1930s. If a surface battle had taken place between the *Iowa* and the *Tirpitz*, most naval analysts agree that the *Iowa* with its superior firepower and Mark 38 main battery director with the Mark 8 fire control radar would have triumphed. The *Tirpitz* was to have been armed with eight 16-inch guns, and with the new Wurzburg radar as part of its fire control, the outcome might have been different. However, a rush to build the *Bismarck* class prevented the ships from being properly armed with 16-inch weapons. The rest is history. *Author's Collection*

The living quarters aboard the heavy cruiser USS *Houston* (CA-30) as designed for President Roosevelt. He often used this cruiser for fishing trips and diplomatic trips in the late 1930s. He was greatly saddened when the *Houston* disappeared in the Battle of Sunda Strait in February 1942. *Author's Collection*

the last several decades of world history might have been quite different. Fortunately, the *Porter*'s warning caused the *Iowa* to evade the speeding torpedo, and events carried on as we know them.

THE PROBLEMS BEGIN

The USS *William D. Porter* was one of many *Fletcher*-class, high-bridge destroyers built during World War II. They were powerful and menacing ships. They mounted a main battery of five dual-purpose, 5-inch 38-caliber guns and an assortment of 20mm and 40mm antiaircraft guns, but their main armament consisted of ten fast-running and accurate torpedoes that carried 500-pound warheads. The *Porter* was placed in commission on July 6, 1943, under the command of Commander Wilfred Walter, a man on the navy's career fast track.

In the months before she was detailed to accompany the *Iowa* across the Atlantic in November 1943, the *Porter* and her crew learned their trade, but not without experiencing certain mishaps that were to set the stage for the "big goof." Actually, the mishaps began when she was mysteriously ordered to escort the *Iowa*, the new pride of the fleet, to North Africa. The night before they left Norfolk, the *Porter* successfully demolished the upperworks of a nearby sister ship when she backed down along its side and, with her anchor, tore down the

The porcelain tub with railings built especially for President Roosevelt aboard the USS *Iowa*. This tub is a one-of-a-kind appointment aboard any U.S. Naval vessel. The photograph is quite rare, and was recently taken by the author. Roosevelt suffered from infantile paralysis and needed support and assistance for bathing. The living quarters, including a separate pantry and cooking facility, were specially modified for Roosevelt's voyage across the Atlantic to his meeting in Teheran with Stalin and Churchill. Later, he rode the *Iowa* back to the United States, and the bathing facilities have been allowed to remain as a piece of naval history. At one time a brass plaque hung on the door leading to the bathing area that stated in part, "PRIVATE BATH–PRESIDENT FRANKLIN DELANO ROOSEVELT . . . November 1943 embarked with Joint Chiefs of Staff . . . and disembarked at Chesapeake Bay on December 16, 1943. . . The USS *Iowa* steamed 8,150 miles at an average speed of 24 knots. His final words to the crew were: 'Good Luck, and remember that I am with you in spirit. Each and every one of you.' " *Author's Collection*

other ship's railings, life rafts, boat, and various other formerly valuable pieces of equipment. The *Willie Dee* merely had a slightly scratched anchor, but her career of mayhem and destruction had begun.

Twenty-four hours later, the four-ship convoy that consisted of the *Iowa* and her secret passengers, the *Porter*, and two other destroyers was under strict instruction to maintain complete silence. As they were going through a known U-boat feeding ground, speed and silence were the best defenses. Suddenly, a tremendous explosion rocked the convoy, and all of the ships commenced anti-submarine maneuvers. The maneuvers continued until the

The USS *William D. Porter* (DD-579), a hard-luck ship if there ever was one. The novice and overanxious captain and crew accidentally fired a live torpedo at the USS *Iowa* on the trip across the Atlantic with some of the leaders of the free world aboard. The *Iowa* was not hit, due to rapid action by its captain. *U.S. Navy*

Porter sheepishly admitted that one of her depth charges had fallen off of the stern and detonated. The safety had not been set as instructed. Captain Walter was watching his fast-track career becoming sidetracked.

Shortly thereafter, a freak wave inundated the *Porter*, stripping away everything that wasn't lashed down; one man was washed overboard and never found. Next, the *Porter*'s engine room lost power in one of its boilers. Along with everything else that had happened, the captain had to make reports almost hourly to the *Iowa* on the *Willie Dee*'s difficulties. At this point, it would have been merciful for the force commander to have detached the hard-luck ship back to Norfolk, but he did not.

JUST WHEN THINGS COULDN'T BE WORSE

The morning of November 14, 1943, dawned with a moderate sea and pleasant weather. As the *Iowa* and her escort were just east of Bermuda, the president and his guests wanted to see how the big ship could defend herself against air attack. So the *Iowa* launched a number of weather balloons to use as antiaircraft targets. It was exciting to see over a hundred guns shooting at the balloons, and the president was duly proud of his navy. Just as proud was Admiral Ernest J. King, the chief of Naval Operations, who was also aboard. Over on the

Willie Dee, Captain Walter watched the fireworks display with admiration and envy. Thinking about career redemption and breaking the hard-luck spell, the captain sent his impatient crew to battle stations, and they began to shoot down the balloons that the *Iowa* had missed and that had drifted into the *Porter*'s vicinity. Down on the torpedo mounts, the crews watched, waited, and prepared to take practice shots at the big battleship, which even at 6,000 yards seemed to blot out the horizon. Lawton Dawson and Tony Fazio, torpedomen, were among those responsible for the torpedoes and ensuring that the primers were installed during actual combat and removed during practice. Dawson, unfortunately, forgot to remove the primer from torpedo tube number three. Up on the bridge, a new torpedo officer ordered the simulated firing and commanded, "Fire one, fire two," and finally, "fire three." There was no "fire four," as the sequence was interrupted by a "whoooossshhh" sound that was the unmistakable noise made by a successfully armed and launched torpedo.

Lieutenant H. Seward Lewis, who witnessed the entire event, saw the torpedo hit the water on its way to the *Iowa* and some of the most prominent figures in world history. He innocently asked the captain, "Did you give permission to fire a torpedo?" Captain Walter

A torpedo being fired from a tube aboard a destroyer. This was like the scene aboard the *William D. Porter* when the torpedo was accidentally loosed on the *Iowa*. *Author's Collection*

uttered something akin to, "Hell no, I, I . . . whatttttt?" (It was not exactly in keeping with other famous naval quotes such as John Paul Jones's "I have not yet begun to fight" or even Farragut's "Damn the torpedoes, full speed ahead," although the latter would have been appropriate.)

The next five minutes aboard the *Willie Dee* consisted of everyone racing around shouting conflicting instructions and attempting to warn the *Iowa* of imminent danger. First, there was a flashing light warning about the torpedo, but indicating the wrong direction. Next, the *William D. Porter* signaled that she was going in reverse at full speed. There was strictly enforced radio silence in effect, but finally it was decided to notify the *Iowa*. The radio operator on the destroyer yelled, "Lion [code word for the *Iowa*], Lion, come right." The *Iowa* operator, more concerned about improper radio procedure, requested that the offending station identify itself first. Finally, the *Iowa* received the message and began turning to avoid the speeding torpedo.

Meantime, on the *Iowa's* bridge, word of the torpedo firing had reached the president, who only wanted to see, and asked that his wheelchair be moved to the railing. His loyal Secret Service bodyguard immediately drew his pistol as if he were going to shoot the torpedo. The *Iowa* began her evasive maneuvers, yet trained all of her guns on the *William D. Porter*. There was now some thought that the *Porter* was part of an assassination plot.

Within moments of the warning, there was a thunderous explosion just behind the battleship. The

The three men who were closest to the "fish that got away" story. Tony Fazio, H. Seward Lewis, and Paul Hudson of the *William D. Porter*. Their 1958 reunion broke the story of the accidental firing of the torpedo at the USS *Iowa*. The author interviewed Fazio and Lewis about the event, and got a blow-by-blow description. For the first fifteen years after the event, the story had been kept quiet, but no longer. *Author's Collection*

The USS *William D. Porter* lists to starboard off Okinawa after a bomb-laden kamikaze explodes under its hull. No one in the crew was killed, and a rescue by LCS-86 on June 10, 1945, saved the day. *Author's Collection*

torpedo was detonated 100 yards aft by the wash kicked up by the battleship's increased speed. The crisis was over, as well as some careers. Captain Walter's final utterance to the *Iowa* was in response to a question about the origin of the torpedo, and the answer was a weak "We did it."

AFTERWARD

Shortly thereafter, the brand-new, state-of-the-art destroyer, her ambitious captain, and seemingly fumbling crew were placed under arrest and sent to Bermuda for trial. It was the first time that an entire ship and her company had been arrested in the history of the United States Navy. The ship was surrounded by marines when it docked in Bermuda and held there for

several days as the closed session inquiry attempted to determine the facts.

The outcome was delayed for a couple of days until torpedoman Dawson finally confessed to having inadvertently left the primer in the torpedo tube, which caused the launching. Just after the torpedo left its tube, Dawson had thrown the primer over the side to conceal his mistake. The truth was eventually pried out of him, and the inquiry drew to a close. The whole incident was chalked up to an incredible set of circumstances and placed under a cloak of secrecy. The navy then behaved like a mother telling her husband when one of the kids had done something wrong, even though accidentally—"Don't just stand there, punish somebody!"

A 5-inch 38-caliber twin mount with two barrels that could put up to twenty shells per minute per gun at the enemy (short duration only). This particular mount is aboard the USS *Missouri*. During kamikaze swarm attacks, the superstructures of the *Iowa*-class battleships almost looked like they were on fire due to the 5-inch guns, 40mm Bofors guns, and the 20mm Oerlikon cannons firing so rapidly. It was a situation where men who wanted to live fought men who wanted to die. *Author's Collection*

Captain Walter and several other former *William D. Porter* officers and sailors eventually found themselves in obscure shore assignments, and Dawson was sentenced to fourteen years at hard labor. President Roosevelt intervened, however, and asked that no punishment be meted out, as it was an accident.

Following a series of further mishaps, including several friendly-fire incidents, the *William D. Porter* was sunk in a kamikaze attack off Okinawa on June 10, 1945. Fortunately, all hands were saved. On occasion, crew members of the *Willie Dee* have gathered together and remembered the ship they served on. They recalled the good times, and as the years pass, the torpedo incident has become one of amusement and notoriety, rather than one of heart-wrenching embarrassment.

THE WAR IN THE PACIFIC

The war in the Pacific was a far greater problem than that of a runaway torpedo and a hard-luck destroyer. The *Iowa* left the president and his party at Casablanca, and when the conference had ended, picked up Roosevelt and returned him to the United States without incident.

On January 2, 1944, the new battleship pointed its bow toward the Panama Canal and westward to where the Japanese were making one last-ditch stand after

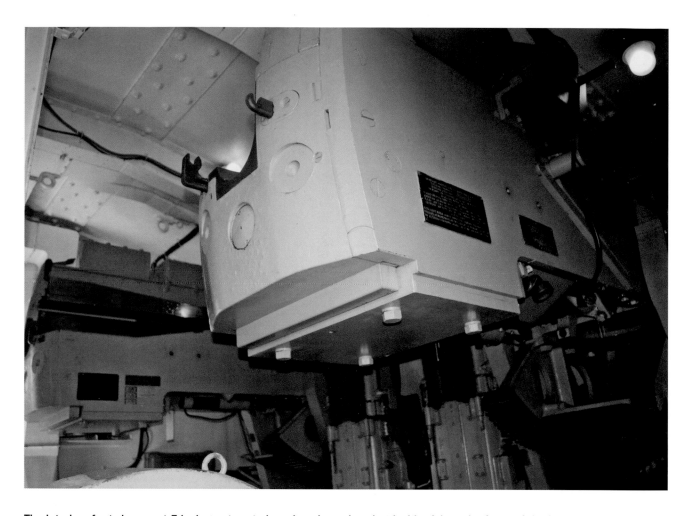

The interior of a twin-mount 5-inch gun turret aboard an *Iowa*-class battleship. A breech of one of the barrels can be seen, and during battle, men would load, fire, and remain out of the continuously moving mount and barrels that were director controlled. The projectile weighed 54 pounds. The heat could reach 130 degrees in the turret, and the crew indeed felt relieved when the battle was finished. *Author's Collection*

another in their crusade to stop the Allied island-hopping strategy toward their homeland. The *Iowa* was appointed flagship of Battleship Division 7, and its next stop was the Marshall Islands. The ship's primary assignment was to support the fast carriers as they made air strikes on various Japanese bases from Kwajalein to Truk in early 1944. In addition to defending the carriers against Japanese retaliation from the air, the *Iowa* and its consorts searched for Japanese warships and support vessels and dispatched them as well.

The drive across the central Pacific was on a strict timetable, and the *Iowa* moved like a freight train. During one of the bombardment runs on Mili Atoll in the Marshalls, the *Iowa* was struck by two 4.7-inch shore battery shells. One detonated on the starboard side of

Turret No. 2, and other hit the armor belt on the hull just below. There were two injured seamen, as the shell that hit the hull opened a small hole in the plating. There was no other damage except that the areas needed new paint.

From this point forward, the *Iowa* was part of a huge juggernaut bearing down on Imperial Japan. From Australia and up through New Guinea, General Douglas MacArthur seemed to be racing against Admiral Chester Nimitz, whose fleet was moving from one island to another across the broad Pacific. Some Japanese-held island fortresses were simply ignored and allowed to wither and die. There was no military sense in wasting men and material on islands that did not contribute to the ultimate goal of having U.S. Army–Air Force bases within range of the homeland. Once the long-range B-29

A quad 40mm Bofors gun aboard a battleship. The *Iowa* class was peppered with quad 40mm guns so that any attacking aircraft could be hit by a number of these well-sited, rapid-fire, four-barrel guns. *Author's Collection*

Super Fortresses could be brought close enough, then cities located on the Japanese home islands would be pounded into submission night after night. Guam, Tinian, and Iwo Jima became critical pieces of real estate that would support the bombers and, later, the P-51 Mustang fighter escorts.

Aside from escorting the fast carriers, the *Iowa* and other fast battleships bombarded Japanese land positions and made periodic antishipping sweeps to destroy Japanese warships and transports. They sought the Japanese navy's remaining battleships without letup.

The *Iowa* assisted in the landings on Leyte Island in the southern Philippines in October 1944, and then escorted the carriers as they bombed Okinawa on the outskirts of the main islands of the empire. The Japanese navy employed nearly all of its surface forces in a final attempt to drive the Allies away from the inner circle of defense, and the *Iowa* was poised for its first real surface action.

Just as the battleship and several American heavy units were about to engage the enemy, word was received that the Battle of Samar was underway between the Japanese central force of battleships, cruisers, and destroyers and a number of jeep carriers and their escorts. Even the famed Japanese battleship *Yamato* was involved. In fact, Admiral Sprague's force of six escort carriers, three destroyers, and four destroyer escorts began to fight it out with a determined but confused force of four battleships, seven heavy and light cruisers, and eleven destroyers. Sprague made smoke, called for help, and then launched everything that could fly at the enemy. His valiant escort did what destroyer men always do: head for the enemy and attack. After a spirited, yet one-sided battle, the Japanese withdrew. They had no effective radar, and the smoke interfered with their ability to determine the American fleet composition. The *Yamato* was leaking badly and was down by the head, so Admiral Takeo Kurita, who was in overall command, decided that the battle was over.

The *Iowa* missed a chance to actually get into a gun duel with its intended opponent, the *Yamato*. However, the sea battles around Leyte Gulf in October of 1944

The mark made by the Japanese 4.7-inch shore battery on Turret No. 2 of the USS *Iowa* on March 18, 1944. A gray painted tape arrow shows the damage to the turret. *Author's Collection*

destroyers. The battleships lobbed 860 16-inch shells at the Nihon Steel Company and Japan's second largest pig-iron and coke factory, the Wanishi Ironworks. Of the shells fired, 170 found the mark within the plant and did horrific damage to this industry. The range was from 28,000 yards to 32,000 yards and proved the value of the fast battleship.

On July 17 and 18, the task unit meted out a like treatment to Hitachi, on Honshu. In essence, the *Iowa* and its consorts had become a littoral-combat, surface-action group and could come well within sight of the Japanese homeland to destroy targets with their main batteries.

THE END OF WORLD WAR II

The *Iowa* accompanied the USS *Missouri* (BB-63) into Tokyo Bay to receive the Japanese surrender on August 29, 1945. Both ships were quietly prepared for anything, and if there was any problem, they could respond with their weapons instantly. The *Iowa* was moored near the *Missouri*, where the surrender ceremonies would take place, and had been assigned as Admiral William F. Halsey's flagship. On September 2 the worst and bloodiest war in human history was ended by a series of pen strokes on a paper. Aboard the *Missouri*, the American flag fluttering from the jackstaff was the same ensign that had flown over the capitol building in Washington on December 7, 1941.

The *Iowa* departed for the United States on September 20.0, 1945, and arrived in Seattle, Washington, on October 15. It was not long before the battleship was back in Japanese home waters and was the flagship of the Fifth Fleet.

For the next four years, the *Iowa* acted as a training ship for reservists. Yet due to the high costs of operation and the lack of a real need for a large number of battleships, the *Iowa* and most other capital ships were decommissioned. The *Iowa*'s turn came on March 24, 1949. Deactivation and the storage of vital equipment were carried out in San Francisco beginning in September 1948, and after decommissioning the ship joined scores of others in the Pacific Reserve Fleet, San Francisco Group. The *Iowa* had served the nation for nearly six years and was worth every penny the taxpayers spent.

After the war, the American public was screaming for appliances and new automobiles, and these items required steel. The best and most plentiful sources of

were the nails in the coffin of the Imperial Japanese Navy. It ceased to exist as a force. It took submarines, older battleships, cruisers, destroyers, and aircraft to finish off what had once been considered the unstoppable Japanese navy, but it was done. The Allies soon took back the Philippines, and the next and final battle was to take Okinawa. This battle would be a dress rehearsal for the attack on the main islands of the Japanese Empire.

The *Iowa* returned to the United States for an overhaul in January 1945 at the Hunters Point Navy Yard in San Francisco, yet was back in the western Pacific and off to Okinawa by April 15, 1945. Aside from escorting the fast carriers and helping to ward off the latest menace, the kamikaze, the *Iowa* joined surface-action groups to bombard the Japanese islands. On July 14 and 15, her 16-inch guns fired continuously at Muroran, Hokkaido, much to the surprise of local people. A task unit under the command of Admiral Oscar C. Badger included the *Iowa, Missouri, Wisconsin*, two light cruisers, and eight

An example of barrage fire by battleships at the Battle of the Santa Cruz Islands on October 26, 1942. In the deep background, the USS *South Dakota* (BB-57) was putting up so much antiaircraft fire that many thought she was on fire. That day, the only carrier left in the Pacific, the USS *Enterprise* (CV-8), at the left of the picture, was saved by this battleship that knocked down twenty-six attackers. *U.S. Navy*

steel were scrapped military vessels. Accordingly, the USS *New Mexico*, USS *Idaho*, and dozens of cruisers, destroyers, and older auxiliary ships were put to the scrapper's torch within months after World War II ended.

Other former Axis countries were also compelled to scrap their fleets (or what was left of them). The Allied nations could no longer afford to maintain large numbers of battleships. By 1960, virtually every older battleship in the world's navies was broken up; only the Soviet Union and United States maintained battleships as potential weapons. (The Soviet battleships were prewar dreadnought vessels and a few decades-old Italian ships granted to their navy by Italian surrender terms.)

By 1960, the U.S. Navy had scrapped all but the museum donations (the *Massachusetts*, *Alabama*, *Texas*, and *North Carolina*) and the four-ship *Iowa* class. Held in reserve to support future operations, the *Iowa*-class vessels now reigned supreme as the most powerful battleships in the world.

Midshipmen identified by the stripe on the white hat spell out NAVY on the deck they are holystoning aboard an *Iowa*-class battleship, the USS *Missouri*. The *Iowa* class was equipped with a deck of Burmese teakwood, which in the twenty-first century is an endangered wood, and if it was not, the cost would be prohibitive. The teak aboard the *Iowa* is rotting and must all be removed, whereas that aboard the *Missouri* is in pristine condition due to proper and regular care. The *Iowa* will probably have its teakwood deck, which is peeling up, replaced by knot-free Douglas fir that has been impregnated with polyethylene. This will cost a minimum of $5.5 million. *U.S. Navy*

The USS *Iowa* makes its way under the San Francisco Bay Bridge in July 1947. The ship is carrying a large number of midshipmen from the U.S. Naval Academy as well as many reservists. The cruise will take them along the California coast and allow them to familiarize themselves with a modern battleship and the latest in electronics. They will also learn some of the more old-fashioned methods of ship care. *Author's Collection*

CHAPTER FIVE

KOREA: 1952

The joy and unrestrained happiness in September 1945, when the Japanese signed the surrender documents on the USS *Missouri*, within sight of the *Iowa*, was abruptly shattered on June 25, 1950. That was the day that the North Korean military crossed into South Korea, and within three days it overran Seoul, the nation's capital. The North Korean forces totaled 110,000 men and a thousand pieces of armor and artillery. Republic of Korea (ROK) military forces and American army units near the border were decimated, and the U.S. Navy and its allies were the only credible force that could be brought to bear reasonably quickly.

Most military analysts recognized the fact that an uncomfortable truce had existed between the West and Soviet bloc nations and their allies. It had begun within weeks of the Japanese surrender and caused an "Iron Curtain" to be drawn between the West and the Soviet-controlled areas in Europe. In the Far East, the same was done, yet the division was termed the Bamboo Curtain. The Western powers settled on a course of action known as containment. In short, Soviet and Communist expansion was not to be permitted to spread into any areas beyond their current control.

South Korea just happened to be the target of choice at that particular time. Would the United Nations and the United States live up to their resolve to protect those nations that embraced democracy and the concept of the U.N.? After all, the small nations now depended on the U.N. to act as an arbitrator and prevent the destruction of war.

There had been mild to moderate challenges within months of the Charter of the United Nations being signed in June 1945. In 1946 and 1947, Soviet-backed Communist rebels attempted to topple the Greek government and later the Turkish government. The battleship USS *Missouri* (BB-63), accompanied by the light cruiser USS *Providence* (CL-82) and destroyer USS *Power* (DD-839), was sent to the eastern Mediterranean to demonstrate clout to the rebels and overt support for the Greek and Turkish peoples. The rebels were defeated, and peace again came to the region.

On the other side of the globe, the jungles of Malaysia became another battleground for homegrown Communist-backed rebels who sought to disrupt the government and terrorize the citizens. British warships, including the frigate HMS *Amethyst*, helped to stomp out

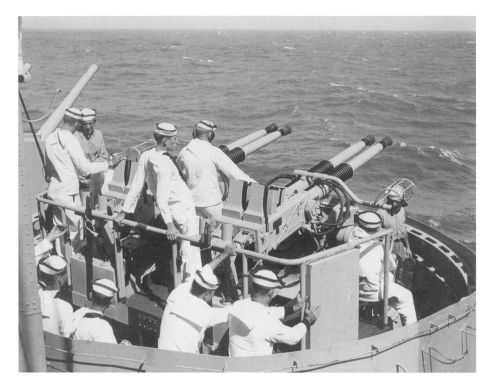

Midshipmen have much more fun firing a 40mm Bofors quad close-in weapons system than holystoning a teakwood deck. There are nine middies assigned to this antiaircraft mount, compared to a Vulcan Phalanx 20mm CIWS, which has one person guiding it below decks. The rest of the work is by computer and radar. The CIWS is far more accurate and less wasteful of ammunition. It took twenty-four thousand 40mm shells to knock down an incoming kamikaze, and the pointer and trainer needed the best eyes aboard ship. In addition, there was very little protection for loading crews in battle. *U.S. Navy*

A stunning image of the *Iowa* as flagship of the Seventh Fleet and carrying Commander, Task Force 77, Vice Admiral Robert Briscoe. Its fixed-wing OS2U-3 Kingfisher and later, high-speed SC-1 Seahawk have been eliminated, as have the catapults. In their place is a rotary-wing aircraft, and one of the first assigned to U.S. Naval vessels—either an HO2 S-1 or an HO3S rescue helo. During its deployment off Korea, the *Iowa*'s helicopter rescued two carrier pilots that had crashed into the cold Pacific. By the end of the Korean War, most capital ships and carriers were equipped with the HO3S. *U.S. Navy*

this scourge. However, the insurgency flared up often between 1948 and 1957.

Czechoslovakia became a bloody killing ground in March 1948 with the Soviet-inspired assassination of the country's leaders. The Soviets quickly followed up the killings by blockading all ground entrances to West Berlin with armored units. The Soviet leadership was willing to risk a European war to enforce this blockade and effect the ultimate starvation of the West Berliners. The Western allies solved this problem during 1948 and 1949 with continuous air deliveries of food, fuel, and other supplies. The Soviet military was eventually embarrassed to the point where a ground blockade was ineffective. The Soviets lifted the blockade and never attempted it again.

Of course, it was just a matter of time before the newest of wars, the Cold War, would turn hot. At first, this new war was geared to stop the North Korean forces from taking all of South Korea. Next, the strategy called for driving the enemy armies back across the 38th Parallel, and keeping them there permanently.

INVOLVEMENT OF THE *IOWA*-CLASS BATTLESHIPS

It was patently obvious that much of the Korean Conflict would be fought from the decks of carriers, amphibious

The USS *Iowa* steams from Pearl Harbor to the battle zone off Korea in 1952. The ship has had some minor modifications and improved electronics installed following the three years she has been in mothballs. *Author's Collection*

ships, and heavy-gun warships fighting in the littoral. The North Koreans and their Chinese and Soviet backers decided to flood the seas around the ports with inexpensive but lethal sea mines. It was estimated that the North Korean military released at least four thousand mines. They floated the mines down streams and rivers to the port cities, dropped them from junks, and utilized any other mine-laying method that was inexpensive. The U.N. minesweeper became an indispensable warship and experienced several losses, as did the destroyers that steamed in the same areas.

As for the battleships, their long-range, 16-inch weapons were invaluable to troops ashore, providing fire support and destroying coastal railways, warehouses, gun batteries, and dozens of other military and industrial targets. By the uneasy end of the Korean Conflict, all of the *Iowa*-class ships—the USS *Missouri* (BB-63), USS *Wisconsin* (BB-64), USS *New Jersey* (BB-62), and, of course, the USS *Iowa* (BB-61)—had been recalled from their reserve anchorages and refurbished for combat. The *Wisconsin* was already in Korean waters and deep into the shooting war when the *Iowa* was to be its replacement. The Korean police action was a highly

opportune way to return the battleships to active service and install updated equipment. At the same time, the *Iowa* class was shorn of its small anti-kamikaze weapons (20mm guns and many of the 40mm quad mounts), which were labor intensive.

The USS *Iowa* had been in mothballs or reserve since its decommissioning on March 24, 1949. It was the navy's policy to put these valuable warships in a state of preservation that would allow them to return to active service with the fleet within weeks. The *Iowa* was recommissioned on August 8, 1951. For the next eight months, its crew acclimated themselves to one another and to the ship as they exercised off the California coast. This area was the same one where reservists and officer candidates had trained on the *Iowa* in the late 1940s, before the battleship was decommissioned. Now the training would pay off.

In March 1952 the *Iowa* pointed its bow toward familiar territory, the western Pacific. The Korean situation began as a police action and now was an outright war, which included one million Chinese soldiers who crossed over into North Korea to assist their ally. Accordingly, the U.S. Navy was compelled to rapidly expand in

An excellent color photo of the *Iowa* at medium speed during the Korean War. Although the majority of the 20mm Oerlikon and 40mm Bofors quad guns have been removed, a few still remain. The fear of propeller-driven aircraft and small enemy attack craft still persisted. The small weapons were also useful against mines. *U.S. Navy*

order to meet this challenge. As soon as the *Iowa* reached the U.S. naval base at Yokosuka, Japan, she was immediately designated as the flagship of the Seventh Fleet. It was an immense responsibility, and Vice Admiral Robert T. Briscoe broke his flag aboard the ship on April 1, 1952. The *Wisconsin* was then able to sail for its home port in the United States.

Admiral Briscoe wasted no time, and by April 8 the *Iowa* was firing on enemy supply routes, warehouses, gun emplacements, and any and every industrial or military target available. Like 80 percent of the world's nations, North Korea maintained its communication, transportation, industrial, and population centers within fifty miles of the coastline. The *Iowa*'s activity was the classic definition of littoral warfare, the type of warfare that in the twenty-first century will dominate naval strategy and tactics.

By mid-April 1952, the *Iowa* was tasked to assist the First ROK Corps during an action against the North Korean army. The ship's guns fired continuously at one target after another. As call-fire missions came, the 16-inch guns roared. Over one hundred troops were killed,

six major gun batteries were destroyed, and the North Korean divisional headquarters was hit hard. The *Iowa* enabled the First ROK Corps to carry out its attack successfully.

Next, the ship moved to Wonsan, where it hit observation posts, warehouses, and railroad marshaling yards. North Korea's primary artery for transporting men and supplies was its rail system. Trains often took the coastal routes and had such nicknames as "the Wonsan Limited." These trains became targets for any United Nations ship, and in particular, the battleships and cruisers. Not to be left out, the destroyers also lay in wait for trains. A club was formed known as the Train Busters, and one of the most prominent members was the *Iowa*. Gunners on the *Iowa* and other bombardment ships often shot up the struts and timbers holding up a trestle or railroad bridge. A train with its heavy weight would collapse the bridge and cascade into the gulch or canyon below.

Another train-busting technique the *Iowa* excelled in was closing vital tunnels with its heavy ordnance. Lookouts aboard the battleship continually searched for tunnels, and when they saw a train racing for the cover of one, the guns concentrated their fire on the other end so the train would collide with the closed exit. To ensure that they were successful in trapping a train, the gun crews then shifted their fire to close the entry. Of course, this tactic was not always successful. On one occasion, a tunnel was sealed at both ends by concentrated 16-inch gunfire, and to ensure that the train was eliminated, the ship's lookouts watched for almost an entire day. They saw smoke lazily drifting out of the exit to the tunnel, which indicated that the train was trapped. Finally, on the third day, the ship's captain became overly curious and, risking capture, dispatched a launch to shore to see what was going on. The boat crew found that the inventive enemy had dug a side tunnel and laid track to allow the train to escape behind the tunnel. Three boys were burning old tires in the tunnel and causing enough smoke to fool the Americans. The boat crew returned to the ship somewhat sheepishly. This type of ingenuity

An amidships look at the *Iowa* in color. The rust from hull-mounted valves and drains is obvious, and the modifications to the bridge are also prevalent. An enclosed armored control room provided excellent protection during a major gun-to-gun duel, but an outside bridge structure provided the captain and his staff with a better view of the ship and what was going on around it. A large number of 40mm quad Bofors mounts are obvious. *U.S. Navy*

was unusual, however. The trains were usually destroyed if found to be on the coastal route.

On May 25, 1952, within forty-eight miles of the Soviet border, the *Iowa* shot up the industrial center at Chongjin, just after closing four railroad tunnels at Tanchon. The *Iowa* was the first visitor this close to the Russian border since the USS *Missouri* (BB-63) pounded targets in the region during November 1950. Three days later, the *Iowa* was back in Wonsan Harbor assisting the U.S. X Corps in its drive northward. The battleship paved the way for the corps by destroying enemy troop concentrations and hitting shore batteries in the harbor.

The battleships, including the *Iowa,* along with several cruisers and destroyers, pounded targets in control of the enemy or in North Korea along the coasts. North Korea's transport system was an ideal target for ship

bombardment. The country's primary rail and roadway system ran along the coast, beginning within a few miles of the Soviet border and within 125 miles of the port of Vladivostok. This Soviet port was a vital, ice-free sea link for Russia. The rail and communication lines began in North Korea's northernmost cities, Ungg and Najin. From there they wound their way some 425 miles south to Yangyang near the 38th Parallel. There were dozens of tunnels, and the trains had to climb through two moderately high mountain ranges. Along the way, cities provided various war materials, supplies, and troops to move southward and to the battlefields. It was vital to disrupt and destroy this supply and communication route. The battleships were perfect for hitting targets up to twenty-five miles inland, and the *Iowa* was continually on the gun line along the coast. Of course, the North Koreans were masters at rebuilding damaged track, trestles, and

A breeches buoy is being used in this image aboard the *Iowa*. The sailor is being transferred back to his ship, the USS *Alfred A. Cunningham* (DD-752), a *Sumner*-class destroyer. This was not a frequent attraction, so the crew turned out en masse to watch. The trick was to keep the ships at the pre-determined distance apart so as not to give the rider a soaking. *U.S. Navy*

bridges, and clearing tunnels. Often, it seemed as if the damage was done in the afternoon, and by the following morning, trains were running again.

The North Korean army established a number of shore batteries to fire upon the smaller warships, and these batteries hit a variety of destroyers and other ships that came within their range. One such ship was the USS *Thompson* (DMS-38). The *Thompson* was originally a *Benson-Livermore*–class destroyer that was rebuilt and reclassified as a fast minesweeper in May 1945. It had three 5-inch 38-caliber guns, and they were used often against the North Korean military. Unfortunately, the *Thompson* was hit on the bridge by a medium-caliber shell from a shore battery near Songjin on June 14, 1952. Three of its crew were killed and three wounded. The *Thompson* had to retire for repairs and treatment of the wounded.

On August 20, 1952, the *Thompson* was again operating off Songjin, and was hit ten times on this occasion. Four of her crew were killed and ten seriously wounded. The *Iowa* was operating within twenty miles of the *Thompson* and immediately came to her assistance. The *Iowa* took off the wounded and covered the *Thompson*'s escape to safer waters. Amazingly, the *Thompson* came back for more, even though she was damaged. She opened fire on targets near Songjin again before departing the area.

(By saving the *Thompson* from the shore batteries of Songjin, the *Iowa* unknowingly made a contribution to great filmmaking. The *Thompson* went on to become a famous movie star. She became a unit in Mine Division 11, and in June 1953 was selected to be the primary prop for the film *The Caine Mutiny*, produced by Columbia Pictures. The film was based on the award-winning book

Another view aft of the *Iowa*. The H03S rescue helicopter can be seen behind the crew who have come up to watch the breeches buoy evolution. The helo replaced the catapult aircraft by the late 1940s, and now can be found on almost all ships. *U.S. Navy*

of the same name, written by Herman Wouk. The *Thompson* worked out of San Francisco during the filming and for several days became the infamous USS *Caine*. Wouk had been a lieutenant junior grade aboard the USS *Zane* [DD-337], which was redesignated DMS-14 in November 1940. He was thoroughly familiar with mine warfare, thus his book and film were adept and accurate reflections of life aboard a destroyer minesweeper [DMS].)

The *Iowa* continued its relentless destruction of the rail centers and any and all military targets. On September 23, 1952, it hit a huge ammunition dump in the Wonsan area, and two days later the 16-inch guns destroyed a thirty-car train complete with engine and coal car near Wonsan.

The *Iowa* was relieved on October 18, 1952, to return to Norfolk for a major overhaul. It had spent 193

days and nights in the battle zone. As long as the *Iowa* was available, she would carry out one mission after another; such was the spirit of this ship and her crew. Even on the day following its relief, the ship was busy shooting at North Korean targets near Koje before leaving for home. It had racked up an enviable record against the enemy and had destroyed thousands of tons of vital supplies, equipment, rolling stock, and trains. For its sterling effort in Korea, the ship earned two battle stars, which it added to the nine stars earned during World War II. The ship made a short stop in Yokosuka, Japan, for minor upkeep, and then sailed for the Norfolk Navy Yard, and a major overhaul.

The battleships again had proved their worth off the coast of Korea and had become the ground soldier's best friend. For a grunt, there is nothing quite as comforting as watching a battleship's one-ton

An HO3S rescue helicopter takes off from an *Iowa*-class battleship. On land and at sea, the helicopter became a major element for rescuing pilots downed at sea and transporting wounded to forward medical units (MASH). Aboard the battleships, the catapults and aircraft were supplanted by rotary-wing aircraft. A helipad was installed on the aft deck for the aviation units. Additionally, radar supplanted the need for a scout aircraft, and the helicopter was a far better aircraft for rescuing downed carrier aircrews. *U.S. Navy*

The USS *Thompson* (DMS-38) at speed. The ship served until May 18, 1954, and then was decommissioned and quickly sold for scrap. As it was of early World War II vintage, there was no purpose in retaining the ship, and no foreign buyers expressed any interest. *Author's Collection*

high-explosive projectiles decimating enemy opposition. The accuracy was phenomenal, especially when the ships were using first-generation analog computers. The four *Iowa*-class battleships destroyed hundreds of commercial, industrial, and military targets in North Korea, as well as continually interrupting train, truck, and troop movements along the coastal route. The North Korean transport system was archaic and depended almost entirely on the labor of humans, so the North Koreans were unable to develop substantial alternate routes during the war. The North Koreans

The USS *Iowa* (BB-61) opens fire on North Korean targets with surprising accuracy in the spring of 1952. Few shore batteries were foolish enough to respond, as their officers knew that the battleship would lay waste to their position and everything surrounding it. Ironically, the gun that is firing is the center barrel in Turret No. 2. Many decades later, this same barrel would figure in the deaths of forty-seven men. *U.S. Navy*

repaired shore-bombardment and bomb damage almost overnight, using thousands of unskilled and semi-skilled men, women, and child laborers. With concentrated 16-inch gunfire, the battleships could destroy the rail marshalling yards with massive explosions. The secondary explosions from ammunition trains would often contribute to the destruction. The battleships did collateral damage to the crude telephone systems, electrical power stations, and commercial building plants.

The battleships made a significant contribution to the war in Korea and helped to bring the Korean

Communist leadership to the peace table. The Korean Conflict came to an uneasy end on July 27, 1953. The United Nations lost 55,440 personnel, and the United States lost 94 percent of that total. (Interestingly, the Battle of Gettysburg during the American Civil War resulted in nearly the same number of casualties in a three-day period.) North Korea lost an estimated six hundred thousand citizens, and China lost one million soldiers. The final armistice returned the line between North and South Korea to the same location as before the war and has been in effect for more than half a century.

A final shoot by the *Iowa* at targets near Koje on October 18, 1952. The battleship was getting in one last hit on the North Koreans despite the fact that the day before was to have been the last day of the battleship's assignment. Its next destination was Pearl Harbor and then to its home port of Norfolk, Virginia. *U.S. Navy*

One of the few images of the entire class of *Iowa* battleships together was taken near Guantanamo Bay, Cuba, in June 1954. The *Iowa*, in the lead, met the other three battle wagons during a midshipmen training cruise. *U.S. Navy*

CHAPTER SIX

IOWA CLASS: 1956–1969

The *Iowa* came home to Norfolk to a rousing welcome from family and friends. The ship was overhauled, new radars were installed, and superfluous antiaircraft weapons removed. A 40mm quad Bofors weapon weighed a respectable 11.5 tons, and there were several still aboard the *Iowa.* Each time the ship came into a shipyard for an overhaul, one or more of the Bofors were removed and stored, and the crew was reduced accordingly. The same was the case with the other three ships in the *Iowa* class. While the rest of the fleet was rearmed with new antiaircraft weapons as needed, the *Iowa*s were not, as they were entering a very long period in reserve.

The leadership in the Department of the Navy now regarded the battleships as a weapon of another era, and it was a waste to rearm them with expensive gun systems. In fact, almost all of the active fleet's cruisers and destroyers had all of their 20mm and 40mm antiaircraft weapons landed long before the battleships did. The cruisers and destroyers now sported radar-controlled twin and single 3-inch 50-caliber rapid-fire weapons as their secondary battery. These guns, as well as the 5-inch 38-caliber twin mounts, could track aircraft flying at up to 350 knots, and

had a reasonable chance of shooting them down. As the Soviets' jet aircraft became faster and more maneuverable, the 3-inch weapons became obsolete, and surface-to-air missiles (SAMs) were then needed to combat them. It always seemed to be a potentially deadly game of one-upmanship with the Soviet armed forces.

In July 1953 the *Iowa* became the flagship of the Second Fleet under Vice Admiral E. T. Woolfidge. In June 1954, during a cruise to Guantanamo Bay, Cuba, with midshipmen from the U.S. Naval Academy, all four *Iowa*-class battleships were in port. Over the next few days, there were a number of one-of-a-kind opportunities to photograph all four operating ships. The *Iowa*s were the only battle line of battleships in the world, as all other nations had disposed of their capital ships.

From late 1954 through 1955, the *Iowa* became the flagship of Commander Battleship, Cruiser Force of the Atlantic Fleet, under Rear Admiral R. E. Libby. During this time, the ship had its main battery guns relined, as the guns were worn out and needed attention to ensure accuracy. During the summer of 1955, the ship had a major update, receiving new electronics and other more modern

Mothballed ships at the Philadelphia Naval Shipyard, in the backwaters of the base's repair and construction activities. Here the USS *Iowa* (BB-61) is moored next to the USS *Wisconsin* (BB-64), and in the distance is the *Essex*-class carrier USS *Shangri-La* (CV-38). The *Shangri-La* was later stricken from the navy's register in 1982. All of the mothballed ships are sealed to prevent humidity, and they are electronically guarded against major hull leaks. *U.S. Navy*

equipment. She was in dry dock and had her hull cleaned and repainted. When the *Iowa* came out of dry dock, she was ostensibly a new ship, yet obsolete compared to most cruisers and destroyers of the time.

INTO RESERVE

It had become obvious that the *Iowa* and her sister ships could not be kept in active service unless there was a definite need for their 16-inch guns or for the size and power of a battleship to impress other nations. As each of the weary *Iowa*s returned from the icy waters off Korea, this fact became even more evident. Because all four battleships were commissioned, over ten thousand officers and men were required, and they had to be fed and cared for. Aside from that expense, the battleships generally

required escorts (destroyers and destroyer escorts) to defend them against Soviet submarines. Therefore, the expense to maintain an *Iowa*-class warship in the fleet was far more costly than maintaining just one ship.

For instance, the crew of each ship consumed seven tons of food per day, including 1.5 tons of fresh food, 2 tons of frozen food, and 3.5 tons of dry food. The storerooms contained 84 tons of frozen meat, 650 tons of dry stores, and a grand total of 834 tons of food to sustain the crew for 119 days. The soda fountain did a roaring business by manufacturing and distributing 9,600 gallons of ice cream per month. (Even the most tattooed and grizzled chief boatswain's mate had a sweet tooth.) A special holiday meal would require 240 gallons of cream of tomato soup, 240 pounds of saltine crackers,

The *Iowa* is anchored at Hampton Roads with a helicopter flying overhead. The battleship was one of America's contributions to the International Naval Review held off Hampton Roads on June 13, 1957. This was an opportunity for nations to display their ships and at the same time foster some degree of cooperativeness. *U.S. Navy*

and 2,849 pounds of turkey. Cigarettes were dirt cheap aboard ship, and the ship's personnel smoked 2,800 packs of cigarettes per day.

Each *Iowa*-class battleship had what amounted to a full-size professional laundry that processed 540,000 pounds of clothing, linen, and other items each month, including 3,600 officers' and chiefs' uniforms, as well as 12,000 pounds of linen.

The barbershop of each ship was also was busy; with eight chairs, it gave 7,400 haircuts per month. The cobbler replaced 650 heels and 250 soles on shoes every month as well. An *Iowa*-class battleship was a small city of 2,500 residents that required the same services as a town, and there was a cost for all of this work. Maintaining these services was an expensive proposition for the taxpayers, and eventually one that the navy could no longer fund. If the battleships were put in reserve, these costs would vanish—a very enticing proposition for those who sought to cut costs in the navy.

The USS *Missouri* was the first of the four to be decommissioned. On February 26, 1955, the *Mighty Mo* went into mothballs at the Puget Sound Naval Shipyard in Bremerton, Washington. The formal designation of the decommissioned ships at this facility was the Pacific Reserve Fleet, Bremerton Group.

Following the *Missouri* was the USS *New Jersey,* which was decommissioned on August 21, 1957, and

moored at Bayonne, New Jersey. Shortly thereafter, the *New Jersey* was moved to the Philadelphia Naval Shipyard, where she remained for eleven years. In 1968, the *New Jersey* was the sole *Iowa*-class battleship to be recommissioned for service in the Vietnam War. Essentially, she performed the same tasks as during the Korean War: shore bombardment and assisting U.S. and allied troops ashore.

The third battleship to be decommissioned was the USS *Iowa*, which was mothballed at the Philadelphia Naval Shipyard on February 24, 1958. She joined the *New Jersey* and remained in quiet reserve for twenty-six years. However, prior to being put in reserve, the *Iowa* was selected to be part of the International Naval Review off Hampton Roads on June 15, 1957. A number of nations sent representative warships to this event, which was periodically held as a display of power and advancement in naval science.

The last of the *Iowa* class to be placed in reserve was the USS *Wisconsin,* which was decommissioned on March 8, 1958. This last decommissioning left the U.S. Navy without a significant capital ship in the active fleet for the first time since the USS *Texas* (BB-000, changed to USS *San Marcos* in 1911) was commissioned on August 15, 1895. The *Wisconsin* was originally placed in Bayonne, New Jersey, yet like the *New Jersey,* it soon moved to the Philadelphia Naval Shipyard to join the

The USS *Iowa* at Suisun Bay in reserve or mothballs. Her hull is protected against corrosion by a cathodic system, and the interior is kept at a constant level of humidity. The ship is anchored and moored fore and aft to prevent any shift from the anchorage, and visitors are strictly prohibited. *Author's Collection*

A 5-inch 38-caliber twin mount on the port side of the USS *Iowa* as of April 2006. It is badly rusted, as is the bulkhead near it. By contrast, the other three *Iowa*-class battleships that are now museum ships have had their surfaces cleaned, sand-blasted, and painted to protect them from further deterioration. This image graphically shows what can happen when a ship is neglected and the weather takes over. *Author's Collection*

Iowa. The *Wisconsin* remained in mothballs from 1958 until it was modernized in the early 1980s.

Over the next few years, a wholesale slaughter of the U.S. Navy's battleships took place, as one after another was scrapped. Rebuilt older battleships—such as the USS *California* (BB-44), USS *Colorado* (BB-43), USS *Maryland* (BB-46), USS *Tennessee* (BB-43), and USS *West Virginia* (BB-48)—were worn out by the late 1950s and thus of no further value. Another group built at the beginning of World War II was also selected for disposition: the USS *Washington* (BB-56), USS *South Dakota* (BB-57), and USS *Indiana* (BB-58) were scrapped, while the USS *North Carolina* (BB-55), USS *Massachusetts* (BB-59), and USS *Alabama* (BB-60) became memorial ships.

A youthful faction in the Pentagon and aboard the newer, missile-dominant warships had gone completely antigun in its planning for future combat at sea. Its members envisioned the missile to be the ultimate naval weapon, and smaller-caliber guns would be used in a secondary role. To this end, they spent an inordinate amount of time and money in research and development.

The captain's cabin aboard the *Iowa* as of April 2006. A pipe crosses the deck as a measure to maintain proper humidity. This room was also once Admiral William Halsey's sitting room as well as that of President Franklin Roosevelt. However, it is now a mess and requires a tremendous amount of work to bring it back to its original condition. *Author's Collection*

The captain's sitting room aboard the USS *Missouri* filmed in March 2006. It is a stark contrast to the sitting room aboard the USS *Iowa. Author's Collection*

Central plot aboard the *Missouri* is highly complex and was installed after the mid 1980s refit. To make the USS *Iowa* a top museum, discerning visitors will accept nothing less than accuracy and the full electronic suite. For years, naval enthusiasts have been glued to the History Channel, and know what is phony. *Author's Collection*

By late 1962, the U.S. Navy, which had previously boasted ten modern battleships with 16-inch-gun main batteries, had been reduced to the four-ship *Iowa* class. The *Iowa*s were also in grave danger of being scrapped, because even in mothballs, the cost to maintain them was in excess of $100,000 per year.

SAVED FROM EXTINCTION

The four *Iowa*s were saved by the recommissioning of the USS *New Jersey* for service in Vietnam 1969. The *New Jersey*'s shore-bombardment role and call-fire assignments for the marines reestablished the value of the heavy gun in the littoral environment. The *New Jersey* spent 120 days on the firing line with other ships and delivered 5,688 16-inch projectiles against shore targets—more than eight times the number it fired during World War II.

Naval analysts woke up to the fact that a battleship could deliver up to 210 tons of ordnance in nine minutes of concentrated fire. It would take an aircraft carrier over twelve hours to launch strike aircraft, recover aircraft, reload, and go through same cycle to achieve what the *New Jersey* could accomplish in nine minutes.

The combat information center (CIC) and radar plot aboard the USS *Missouri*. The compartment should resemble that of the *Iowa* after the *Iowa* has been returned to her original condition. The docents and volunteers aboard the *Missouri* had a very difficult time putting together all of the equipment shown in this image. Some had to be manufactured from scratch, as the original equipment had been thrown out or stolen by "midnight auto supply." Creating a historically accurate ship museum is extremely difficult and time consuming. *Author's Collection*

The *Iowa* is seen entering a dry dock for a periodic cleaning and hull repainting. This was on August 2, 1962, after the ship had been in mothballs for over four years. This also afforded an opportunity to inspect the hull for plate thinning or pitting. *Author's Collection*

And, with forward observers, the battleship's accuracy level could be instantly upgraded. The tactical missiles of the late 1960s were not even able to compete with the effectiveness of the battleship guns. The whiz kids in the Pentagon were unable to convince the chief of naval operations to dispose of the all-gun battleships of the *Iowa* class because the marines categorically said "no" to junking them. Thus the achievements of the *New Jersey* saved the *Iowa* class from being sent to the ship breakers.

A shell lobbed from the *New Jersey* strikes a North Vietnamese target. This is why the *New Jersey* was recalled. Its 16-inch rifles made a great deal of difference to the ground-pounding soldiers who fought the Viet Cong or regular North Vietnamese Army daily. *U.S. Navy*

The four huge battleships remained in reserve and mothballs for decades. Like other ships, they had nylon fishing line stretched over certain areas to keep the seagulls and other birds from defecating on them, and various other means were used to protect them from the elements and wildlife.

The preservation system was scientifically developed to keep water, mold, and high levels of humidity out of the ships. The smaller guns were encased with igloolike enclosures, and plastic spray was shot all over other items, such as radar antennas and gun directors. Many objects were removed and placed inside the ship, and copious notes were taken to record what they were and where their locations were on deck. To preserve the hull, an electrochemical process known as cathodic protection was used to drastically slow corrosion of the underwater hull area. And one of the most important protective measures was ensuring that everything was properly oiled, greased, and painted inside the ship.

In the years that followed World War II, the National Reserve Defense Fleet (NRDF) mothballed $13 billion in American warships and fleet train ships at the cost of $100 million per year. This was a real bargain. At one time, the NRDF had a total of 2,277 ships located in anchorages all over the United States. The NRDF's collection of ships was the single most expensive asset owned by the American people, and the ships were well cared for. On several occasions, however, many of the ships were culled out for:

• Sale or transfer to friendly nations

The USS *New Jersey* is in a dry dock in 1967 to begin preparing the ship for service in Vietnam. As can be seen, the hull has been painted with anti-fouling paint, and scaffolding is on the decks to begin making the changes to the superstructure. The 40mm quad Bofors will all be removed, and new radar and electronics will be installed. *Author's Collection*

- Return to the fleet for active service in the U.S. Navy
- Use by the Department of Agriculture for storage of excess wheat
- Sale or gift to states and cities as memorial ships
- Cannibalization for parts for the active U.S. fleet or foreign fleets (For example, the bow of partially built *Iowa*-class battleship *Kentucky* was grafted onto the USS *Wisconsin* after a collision with the destroyer USS *Eaton* [DD-510] on May 6 1955.)
- Target practice (sinking exercises, or SINKEX) or for

use by other federal or state agencies.

The *Iowa*-class battleships were generally left alone, except for the USS *New Jersey*. Although the *New Jersey* performed well in Vietnam, her next tour of duty would not be until 1982.

As to the other *Iowa*-class ships, they were upgraded to a reasonable level during their hiatus. However, the Soviet navy was quickly developing a blue-water navy to challenge the United States and NATO at sea. The *Iowa* class would again be needed for one-upmanship.

The *Kirov*-class *Admiral Lazarev* (ex-*Frunze*) at speed, from an aft vantage point. The hangar deck has a Kamov Ka-27 Helix anti-submarine warfare (ASW) helicopter about to be struck below with two other rotary wing aircraft. The 5.1-inch 70-caliber automatic twin-barrel dual-purpose gun sits above the helo deck. It can fire up to eighty 59.5-pound rounds per minute and has a range of 16 miles with a reasonable degree of accuracy. *Author's Collection*

CHAPTER SEVEN

THE *KIROV* CLASS: A SOVIET MENACE

The U.S. Navy was without a battleship in its fleet after December 16, 1969, when the USS *New Jersey* (BB-62) was decommissioned for the third time. She had served the navy well off Vietnam, and after being overhauled it was assumed that the ship would return to Vietnam for another tour. But it was not to be, due to a number of reasons, including high cost. The *New Jersey* was put back into reserve at the Puget Sound Naval Shipyard in Bremerton, Washington.

Opposite the *New Jersey* was the USS *Missouri,* which had been moored at Puget Sound since February 26, 1955, and the other two *Iowa*s were moored in reserve on the East Coast. It seemed to be the end of the battleships' sovereignty at sea. Almost everyone who drove by the anchorages knew that the battleship had little or no value in the world's navies. But although there was a lot of talk about disposing of them, few in Congress wanted to do away with the giant decorated veterans completely. As a consequence, the battleships soldiered on and were not disturbed. Then, in the mid-1970s, disturbing news slowly leaked out of the Soviet Union.

The Soviet navy was determined to compete with the U.S. Navy and its NATO allies at sea. To do this, the Soviets had to build a large, modern, and powerful navy. The Soviets also built some of the largest and heaviest-armed ships, train crews, and expanded bases to accommodate the new ships. Soviet naval forces required:

- Missile cruisers with rotary-wing capability and long-range antiship missiles
- Missile battle cruisers with antiship missiles that were capable of competing with the *Iowa*-class battleships and carrier battle groups (CBG)
- Heavy destroyers with gun and missile armament
- Helicopter carriers for anti-submarine warfare (ASW) and amphibious work
- Amphibious ships similar to the U.S. Navy's LSTs (tank landing ships), LSDs (dock landing ships), and LPHs (amphibious assault ships)
- Frigates with blue-water capability
- Aircraft carriers equipped for fixed-wing jump-jet vertical takeoff and landing (VTOL) and conventional takeoff and landing (CTOL)
- Special operations craft and modern patrol boats.

The Soviet navy, under the tutelage of Admiral of the Fleet Sergey Gorshkov, had grown from a junkyard fleet of castoffs from Italy and other navies in 1955 to a credible

1 - Towed sonar
2 - Helicopter deck
3 - SA-N-9 launchers
4 - 5.1-inch (130-mm) twin turret
5 - 30-mm AK 630 multi-barrel
    guns (6x1)
6 - Kite Screech radar

7 - RBU 1000 RL
8 - Top Dome radar
9 - Bass Tilt radar
10 - Top Steer radar
11 - Tin Man optronic system
12 - Round House
13 - Top Pair radar

14 - Low Ball
15 - Palm Frond radar
16 - SA-N-4 launcher
17 - Pop Group radar
18 - SS-N-19 launcher
19 - SA-N-6 launcher
20 - RBU 6000 RL

A diagram of the more important features of the *Kirov*-class nuclear battle cruiser. *Author's Collection*

force by 1970. Gorshkov had been responsible for ridding the navy of its hidebound officers and archaic theories of naval science. He also was responsible for the wholesale scrapping of warships that were of no value in modern warfare. His entire strategic naval philosophy was summed up in a statement that he made about his navy: "The Flag of the Soviet navy flies over the oceans of the world. Sooner or later the United States will have to understand it no longer has mastery of the seas." This statement provided even the least adept with a political and military roadmap to the Soviet navy's direction.

The head of the Soviet state, Joseph Stalin, had always wanted an impressive navy, and knew the worth of naval forces when creating a powerful nation that commanded respect in the world. Gorshkov was also a supporter of this school and studied Alfred Thayer Mahan and other leading naval theorists.

The Baltic Naval Shipyard in St. Petersburg, Russia. This is just a part of the yard, and the dry dock has a local patrol craft in it for general overhaul. The shed in the background is for workers to build ships during the harsh winter months. *Author's Collection*

A *Kirov*-class battle cruiser under construction in Leningrad (now St. Petersburg). The oil-fired steam plant is integrated with the conning tower and radar antennas similar to the American "mack" (combined mast and stack). These images came from a video tape illegally taken by a worker and smuggled out. Today, the photograph is of a relic rather than of something revolutionary. *U.S. Navy*

In 1955, when the battleship *Novorossiysk* struck a moored World War II German ground mine and sank, forward thinkers in the Soviet navy knew the time had come to make major changes. Leading the pack was the youthful, forty-five-year-old Gorshkov. In 1941, at the age of thirty-one, Gorshkov's leadership had helped stop the German army some thirty miles from the outskirts of Moscow and earned him a promotion to flag rank. He also had command of small, well-armed craft that harried the Germans on lakes and rivers. He later assumed command of the Black Sea fleet, dominating that body of water to drive out the Germans. For these and other victories, he was rewarded with the command of the Soviet navy before he turned thirty-five. At war's end, he

worked closely with Stalin, who had great trust in this young man. Together they agreed that the navy should not be burdened with worthless and ancient warships that drained the state treasury.

After Stalin died in 1953, Nikita Khrushchev became the head of the state, and in time, he came to agree with Stalin's naval policy. At the same time, he developed a healthy respect for Gorshkov and his maritime and naval theories.

At first, the Soviet premier was content to expand the navy with small, missile-bearing craft and a substantial submarine force. As early as 1954, he put an end to the construction of twenty-four *Sverdlov*-class light cruisers that were actually inferior to the American *Cleveland* class,

Looking from the bow of a *Kirov*-class battle cruiser aft over the vertical launch system (VLS) for the SS-N-19 Shipwreck missiles, with silo hatches open. It is significant that U.S. Navy cruisers and destroyers as well as newer littoral combat ships have all been or will be armed with the VLS silo for housing and launching missiles. *U.S. Navy*

an early 1940s design with twelve 6-inch guns in the main battery. The Soviet shipyards stopped construction at the fourteenth cruiser and switched to littoral-type craft to guard the fatherland from American amphibious assaults.

At this point, the U.S. Navy and its Western allies in NATO sensed that the next all-out war would be fought with a combination of tactical nuclear weapons and conventional forces. The West also mistakenly believed that the Soviet navy was building a 1,200-boat submarine force that was positioned in layers to defend the Soviet homeland. The outer ring was designed for the long-range attack submarines and missile craft. The medium layer was slightly less capable, but able to engage amphibious and carrier battle groups. The inner ring consisted of the largest number of craft, which were essentially coastal patrol boats that would torpedo the remnants of the Western attack force. The basic plan of defense was simplistic and did not take many contingencies into consideration. For one thing, the Western forces had no intention of repeating a 1944 D-Day operation against the Soviet Union. For another, they had developed rather competent anti-submarine warfare techniques and craft to defeat the layered defenses. By 1960, the U.S. Navy had a large number of superior nuclear attack submarines that were capable of overwhelming the Soviet submarine threat.

Aside from the American submarine forces, the surface ships in the West were quite capable. The West had already placed its *Sverdlov*-equivalent type of ship in reserve, sold six to South American nations, and rearmed some of them with surface-to-air missiles. The West also had over a score of up-to-date aircraft carriers that operated jets of all sizes; heavy cruisers; and even battleships.

By 1960, the West had already scrapped its older battleships, cruisers, destroyers, and smaller aircraft carriers, not to mention the World War II submarines that had not been upgraded to Greater Underwater Propulsion Program (GUPPY) standards. Several of the American World War II *Sumner*-, *Fletcher*-, and *Gearing*-class destroyers were thoroughly modernized all the way down to the main deck in what was known as the Fleet Rehabilitation and Modernization (FRAM) plan. FRAM involved modernizing 131 ships for a cost of $1.233 billion. In general, the ships were rebuilt to fight and sink Soviet submarines. These ships received the most advanced detection gear, as well as ASROCs (rocket-propelled homing torpedoes) and the three-tube Mark 32 ASW homing-torpedo system. Many of these triple-tube lightweight homing torpedoes are aboard ships worldwide into the twenty-first century. Both systems relied upon a detection system that was reasonably accurate, and torpedoes that included nuclear warheads. Compared to the destroyers of World War II, the FRAM destroyers were light years ahead.

Gorshkov was eventually compelled to approach the Soviet leadership and solicit larger cruisers, destroyers, and helicopter carriers that could fire ship-and-task-force–killing missiles at approaching Western carrier and amphibious battle groups. These improvements also meant a complete departure from the navy's avowed policy of its surface forces remaining in coastal waters. Khrushchev and the Soviet Politburo agreed with Gorshkov, and soon several new ship classes were on the drawing board. These included long-range destroyers of the 5,500-ton *Kashin* class; 7,500-ton *Sovremenny*-class destroyers with SAM missiles and an ASW helicopter; and the *Kresta I* and *Kresta II* 7,500-ton cruisers that boasted two missile systems, medium automatic guns, and ASW helicopters. Also proposed and considered

were the 37,000-ton aircraft carrier *Kiev*, which carried thirty-five YAK Forger VTOL fighters and K-25 Hormone helicopters, and the revolutionary 24,300-ton full load *Kirov*-class nuclear battle cruiser. Many in the Soviet navy felt that the battle cruiser was a foolish move backward and openly opposed those who supported it. However, those who believed in the *Kirov* won the day with a singular argument.

The U.S. Navy depended on its aircraft carriers—powered by fossil fuel and, increasingly, nuclear energy—to defend the West and overwhelm any Soviet defenses. With the various missile cruisers (which would include the nuclear-powered, 10,150-ton full load *California* and

The aft 5.1-inch 70-caliber twin mount behind the helicopter hangar on a *Kirov*-class battle cruiser. Above the 130mm gun is a large number of electronic antennas and fire-control apparatus for the guns and missiles. *U.S. Navy*

The aft part of a *Kirov*-class battle cruiser. A helicopter is emerging from the hangar below the 130mm twin mount, and the helipad is just aft of the hangar doors. *U.S. Navy*

the 11,000-ton full load *Virginia* class) supporting the carriers and the large-deck amphibious helicopter-assault carriers, the Soviet Union was in grave danger. It required a class of large, modern, nuclear-power-assisted cruisers that could make over 32 knots and employ the powerful Granit antiship missile structure. This structure consisted of a vertical launch system (VLS) with the highly destructive SS-N-19 P-500 Granit or NATO-dubbed "Shipwreck" missile under one of twenty hatches in the deck. The Shipwreck missile was the kind carried by the Soviet guided-missile submarine *Kursk*, and one or more of these warheads exploding may have contributed to its loss. The SS-N-19 had the option of a 750-kilogram high-explosive (HE) warhead, fuel-air explosive (FAE) payload, or a 500-kiloton nuclear weapon (although the latter weapon option would never be carried).

The *Kirov* class was finally approved, and design began for a four-ship class known as the Type 1144 Kirov in 1970. It was not long before NATO became aware of its existence, and some of the images in this book were taken by an espionage agent using a small video camera.

THE *KIROV* CLASS

The Soviet project to design and build a nuclear battle cruiser was designated Project 1144.2 Orlan (or Sea Eagle). The lead ship was conceived in the very late 1960s, designed in 1970, and laid down in June 1973. It was constructed in the Baltiysky Zavod, or Baltic Naval Shipyard, located in St. Petersburg, formerly Leningrad.

(When the nation rejected Communism in 1990–1991 and returned to the name of Russia, St. Petersburg, the summer home of the czars, again resumed its centuries-old name.) The city is beautiful, and its palaces and museums make it a popular tourist destination. The shipyard was located on one of the canals among the islands around the city. Aside from shipyards, the city also has various naval specialty schools and naval officers' schools for higher learning. The senior officers' school is somewhat akin to the U.S. Navy's War College, and naval personnel can be seen at ships and restaurants all over the downtown area.

The Baltic Shipyard has built 211 commercial vessels and 306 warships since being founded two centuries ago, and most recently completed three 3,780-ton missile frigates for the Indian navy. These are the *Talwar*-class, or Russian Project 11356, missile frigates, which carry Ka-28 Helix rotary-wing aircraft. They entered service for the Indian government in late 2003. There was some financial difficulty as the shipyard was without funding, but this was eventually resolved. This shipyard is now one of three in Russia capable of building warships, although the quality of its ships and workmanship does not compare with that of American and other European yards.

In the early 1970s, secrecy was crucial, and the Soviet state contracted four nuclear-powered battle cruisers with the class name of *Kirov*, celebrating a Bolshevik hero, Sergey Kirov. The official name was summarily dropped for political reasons and replaced by *Admiral Ushakov*, but the nickname *Kirov* seemed to stick. According to NATO, these ships were code-named *Balcom I*, a short version of *Baltic Combatant I*. At first, there was some disbelief that any nation would revert to a surface battle cruiser as one of its primary fighting ships. Of course, the Soviet Union coveted a place at the ever-shrinking table of nations with a credible blue-water capability and the ships to back it up. The Soviets dreamed that a 28,000-ton ship—814 feet long with a 93-foot beam and festooned with a variety of missiles, many of which were in VLS mode—would be the largest, most lethal surface ship extant, aside from an aircraft carrier.

It was not simply wanting the biggest warships that motivated the Soviet state; it was also the desire to add another and very potent method of protecting the fatherland against NATO and the Western powers, with emphasis on the decadent United States. The addition of nuclear power to the *Kirov*'s power plant gave it and its

The *Kirov*, with its forward-mounted VLS silos for its main-battery missiles. *U.S. Navy*

three sisters longer ranges at high speed (up to 14,000 miles at 30 knots), more electrical capacity, and 32 knots or more of surge power.

The intended targets for the *Kirov* class were the NATO amphibious battle groups, especially the big-deck helicopter-attack carriers such as the U.S. Navy's *Tarawa* class (LHA-1), which could launch forty or more helicopters. Also fair game were any serious amphibious assault craft, such as the *Austin*-class LPD; the *Iwo Jima* helicopter carrier; and a variety of other amphibious ships capable of carrying four to thirty helicopters and waterborne landing craft. Other targets included the British *Invincible*-class vertical/short takeoff (V/STOL) carrier with Sea Harrier fixed-wing aircraft and Sea King helicopters.

The *Kirov*'s greatest-priority targets were the aircraft carriers of the nuclear *Nimitz* and *Enterprise* classes, as well as the *Forrestal* and *Improved Forrestal* classes of super carriers. Other fossil-fuel carriers that would be intended targets were the *Midway* class and the older *Essex*-class 34,000-ton ships. The Soviet military and political machine was deathly afraid of another 1941-type attack on the fatherland, and was going to employ

any and all means to prevent a reoccurrence. So it needed ships of extreme capability far at sea to stop any possible attack. For this reason, it built up its nuclear-attack, guided-missile, and ballistic-missile submarine forces, in addition to quickly expanding its surface fleet.

The surface fleet now included the *Kirov*-class nuclear battle cruiser, which was armed with the most advanced missiles available. Of significance was the fact that most of the ships did not carry reloads; thus, the fleet was termed the "one-shot fleet." The philosophy was to fire every weapon and destroy as much of the NATO and Western attacking force on the first, and perhaps the only, exchange of missiles. Of course, the *Kirov*s and other cruisers, destroyers, and frigates were also assigned to destroy enemy submarines and aircraft that were seeking to harm the fatherland.

To this end, the *Kirov* class was armed with a main battery of twenty SS-N-19 Shipwreck missiles that could be guided by the Bear D long-range aircraft and the ship's helicopters using the "Big Bulge" radar system for mid-range guidance. This guidance capability would give this weapon, which had a warhead of either 500

The *Kirov*-class battle cruiser *Admiral Nakhimov*. Originally named the *Kalinin*, she entered service in 1988 and was part of the Northern Fleet. This particular ship was one of the best constructed of its class. Most of the *Kirovs* have been decommissioned, and all will likely be scrapped or towed to the backwaters near Murmansk in the future. There they will be allowed to rot out of camera's view. *U.S. Navy*

kilotons nuclear or 750 pounds of high explosives, a range of 243 nautical miles. The missiles literally played follow the leader. When the first missile was shot down or disabled, another missile would assume the role of leader, and following missiles would dutifully take up station. This action would continue until only one missile remained. It was as if a pre-planned command structure had been built into the missile system.

The *Kirov* class also had the latest in electronic surveillance and guidance radar paired to SA-N-6 Grumble VLS missiles, SA-N-4 Gecko missiles, and SA-N-9 Gauntlet missiles. For offensive antiship torpedoes, the *Kirovs* had two quintuple sets of tubes that could fire 21-inch or 533mm Type E53 torpedoes. These were capable of 40 knots up to 8.1 miles and carried a 1,102-pound high-explosive warhead. As anti-submarine weapons, they could carry a 5-kiloton nuclear warhead. These *Kirov* ships were also armed with close-in weapons systems (CIWS) and anti-submarine weapons for self-protection and for protecting accompanying ships.

Overall, they were potent warships, but it was far too long from conception to commissioning—almost fifteen years. By that time, all four *Iowa*-class battleships were well on the way to being recommissioned, and modern American nuclear cruisers were being built. In essence, the *Kirov* class was too little and too late to be of any real service, except to get the U.S. Navy into the expansion mode

for President Ronald Reagan's much touted six-hundred-ship navy. Besides, the four *Kirov*-class battle cruisers were no match for an *Iowa*-class battleship that had the advantages of the upgrades available in the 1980s.

EPILOGUE FOR THE BATTLE CRUISER

From the outset, British Admiral Jackie Fisher's notion of the battle cruiser was worthless as a naval asset. It depended on speed to outrun its adversary and armament to defeat its contemporary. Unfortunately, this type ship could not outrun heavy-caliber shells or aircraft, and they were its undoing. The litany of battle cruisers lost is a parade of failures dating back to the early 1900s and spanning two World Wars.

As to the *Kirov*, it may have had tremendous firepower, but NATO aircraft would have punctured its defenses long before it had an opportunity to bring its main armament into battle. These ships were poorly built; shipyard bills for services went unpaid; and the collapse of the Soviet Union brought the entire *Kirov* concept to naught. As of the early twenty-first century, only two are able to put to sea, and then only periodically. Even Russian and Ukrainian flag officers consider them marginal warships at best and near death traps at worst. Many in the Russian naval command expect one of the *Kirov* class to blow up at any time due to a number of deficiencies in engineering, weapons, and hundreds of vital missing parts stolen

The Kamov Ka-27, dubbed the "Helix" by NATO. It is flown by Russia, Ukraine, South Korea, Vietnam, China, and India. It first flew in 1974, and the navalized version is for anti-submarine warfare work and for mid-range guidance control for the *Kirov's* Shipwreck missiles. It replaced the Hormone helicopter which had been quite popular in the Soviet Navy. The *Kirov* carried three of the Helix helicopters. *U.S. Navy*

by gangs that work in tandem with Russian naval officers seeking to turn a profit. The ships' nuclear power plants are defective and unsafe. In 2005, the commander-in-chief of the Russian navy was quoted as saying that the nuclear power plant on the *Kirov*-class *Peter Velikiy* made the ship a death trap. The *CONAS* system, which is a combined oil-fired steam and nuclear plant, is supposedly able to generate some 140,000 horsepower; however, the plant has never worked properly and has often breeched basic safety measures.

Like the *Kirov*s, the Oscar II SSGN submarine *Kursk* carried the infamous Granit SS-N-19 Shipwreck missiles. One or more of these weapons may have figured in

the explosion of the forward half of the guided-missile submarine on August 12, 2000. All of the crew was killed. Ironically, the flagship for the *Kursk* recovery effort was the *Peter Velikiy*. The *Kirov* class would never have stood up to the NATO and Western naval forces, and was merely a shadow of a surface ship. The Soviet navy would have been far better off to avoid such a costly and ineffective attempt at grafting a failed early-twentieth-century naval design with a failing late-twentieth-century design. It is probable that the remaining two *Kirov*-class ships will be recycled and sold for scrap within the next five years, and the Soviet and Russian navy's experiment, and embarrassment, will be over.

The USS *Iowa* inbound to her homeport of Norfolk, Virginia, on April 5, 1985. Her starboard crane is out and prepared to receive fuel. It appears as if most of the crew that is not on duty is out on the bridge watching as the ship returns home. This is an excellent view of three of the four 20mm Phalanx CIWS "last-ditch-stand" guns that would protect the "Big Stick," as the *Iowa* was nicknamed. *U.S. Navy*

CHAPTER EIGHT

THE *IOWA* CLASS OF THE 1980S

The brinksmanship game between the United States military and that of the Soviet Union extended to any and all weapons. To the common citizen, this translated to nuclear weapons, bombers, and intercontinental ballistic missiles. The much-feared missiles could be launched from secret silos and roving submarines of incredible size, and detonate in Moscow, Kiev, Chicago, and New York within minutes. Up to four (and perhaps more) warheads would explode above each target at predetermined heights. The targets would be population, industrial, and military centers, and the weapons were designed to destroy as much as possible as well as instill absolute fear. There would be little warning, and millions of people would be killed instantly. For proof of the devastation, people needed only to visit Nagasaki or Hiroshima, Japan, to see what the earliest of atomic weapons could accomplish. The nuclear weapons had since become thermonuclear and far more deadly. They still had the collateral death threat of radiation poisoning; those who were exposed to the fallout of the bomb or the bomb itself, and were not killed by the firestorm, had only a few days or weeks to live, as radiation poisoning would soon set in, and there was (and is) no cure for it. Death from this aspect of nuclear war is sure and certain.

Weapons of the 1970s and 1980s had become phenomenally more potent and destructive than the crude, heavy bombs of the 1940s. They were also much smaller and weighed far less than the original weapons, and thus could be carried on small missiles and much smaller aircraft than the B-29 Flying Fortress of World War II.

There was a time when an exchange of nuclear weapons between the United States and the Soviet Union seemed inevitable, although the thought of how such a war would unfold was beyond comprehension. One popular idea among experts had the war beginning with conventional, non-nuclear forces fighting until a stalemate required escalation to bigger and better weaponry. The losing side would eventually employ tactical nuclear weapons to even the strengths of the combatants. There also was the possibility that nations would employ massive numbers of nuclear weapons in a first strike.

The superpowers had the nuclear weapons and delivery systems to ravage their enemies. And when in 1970 the

The crane on the starboard side enabled fueling with far greater ease. To the left is one of the armored box launchers (ABLs) for the Tomahawk missiles. At one level above the main deck is one of the six twin-mount 5-inch 38-caliber guns in the secondary battery. The difference in gray paint is due to a contract stoppage when the navy decided not to pursue any further repairs to the ship. Legislation sponsored by Representative Richard Pombo effectively took the ship from the navy's responsibility and allowed it to be donated to the Port of Stockton. This has now been revoked, yet the legislation will cost any prospective organization an extra $15 million to continue mandatory refurbishing. *Author's Collection*

Soviet navy elected to build the *Kirov*-class battle cruisers, the international naval community was stunned. How could a navy that was building modern, first-class warships elect to build warships that were of a bygone era? The international community's first response to an 814-foot, nuclear-power-assisted battle cruiser was one of amazement rather than admiration.

(Of course, the Soviets had done the same thing in the early 1950s when they introduced and built fourteen out of twenty-four authorized *Sverdlov*-class light cruisers with a main armament of twelve 6-inch guns. In the United States Navy and Royal Navy, this type of light cruiser was in reserve or being sold to bidder nations, and most of the remaining examples would soon be scrapped. Even Khrushchev claimed that the only thing they were good for was transporting diplomats and state leaders from nation to nation.)

However, as the years went on, it became evident that the *Kirov* class would end up being the largest and most dominant surface ship in the world. With its twenty SS-N-19 Shipwreck missiles, capable of carrying formidable conventional high explosives or small nuclear warheads, the four ships in this class were designed to do great damage to carrier and amphibious battle groups.

Two of the eight Mark 143 ABLs, on the starboard side of the *Iowa*. Each contained up to four Tomahawk missiles. In the foreground to the left is a bracket for holding watertight canisters for the Harpoon antiship missiles. This area has been painted aboard the *Iowa*, but very little else below this level has received new paint. *Author's Collection*

Ingalls Shipbuilding at Pascagoula, Mississippi, where the *Iowa* was in the final stages of being reactivated. The date is September 23, 1983, and to the lower left is the armored conning tower where the ship would be conned during a full battle engagement. The Mark 38 main battery director is turned to port, and the Mark 37 directors for the 5-inch 38-caliber guns have yet to be installed. *U.S. Navy*

A Tomahawk land-attack missile, or TLAM, is launched from the *Iowa* out of one of the starboard ABLs. After the missile is boosted from the ship, it enters a pre-programmed cruise format and can fly over 2,000 miles, depending on the mission and warhead. The Tomahawk has enabled the battleship to fight its enemies at distances far beyond the horizon. During the Gulf War in 1991, the *Missouri* fired 759 16-inch projectiles and 28 Tomahawk missiles. The *Wisconsin* fired 24 Tomahawk missiles at targets in Baghdad and other areas. The 52 Tomahawk missiles fired by the battleships represented 18 percent of the total cruise missiles fired during the war. *U.S. Navy*

Defensive chaff dispensers to simulate the battleship *Iowa*. This is part of the last-ditch stand to help defend the ship against radar-guided enemy missiles. *Author's Collection*

There were no ships in the active fleets of NATO or Western navies that were the same size as the *Kirov*s or packed the same offensive punch.

But there were, of course, four *Iowa*-class battleships sitting in reserve.

KIROV VERSUS IOWA: CHECKMATE

The only ship of the *Iowa* class that had seen active service since the Korean War (1950–1953) was the USS *New Jersey* (BB-62), which was modernized and recommissioned for 120 days of shore bombardment work off the Vietnamese coast in 1968 and 1969. The award for longevity in reserve was the USS *Missouri* (BB-63), which had been inactive since February 26, 1955. She was recommissioned on May 10, 1986, thus had been in reserve for thirty-one years. She had almost become a permanent attraction in Bremerton, Washington, and many felt that when the ship was made available for museum donation, it would go to that city. (Later, a group in Bremerton competed strongly with San Francisco and Pearl Harbor to have the ship as a memorial based in their region, yet Pearl Harbor presented the best and most compelling argument. Moored on "Battleship Row," with the USS *Arizona*, the *Missouri* was the perfect historical bookend to World War II.) But before that, the *Missouri* was needed for two more wars, the ongoing Cold War and the abortive Persian Gulf War.

Initially, there was considerable argument that all of the battleships would serve the country better by being scrapped for tons of excellent, high-tensile steel. The same anti-battleship crowd that had argued against the remaining *Iowa* class in the 1950s was again beating the drums to get rid of the old battleships. It

An RGM-84D Block II Harpoon is launched from a destroyer. The modern Harpoon can distinguish between a land mass, enemy vessel, or neutral shipping. This weapon can be launched from surface ships, submarines, and aircraft, and has a speed of 646 miles per hour, with an effective range of 85 nautical miles. The Harpoon has been a staple in the U.S. Navy's missile inventory since 1977. It is boosted from the canister by a solid propellant, and then carried to the target by a turbojet. The *Iowa* class had sixteen ready-to-fire *Harpoon* missiles. *U.S. Navy*

A contemporary (2006) CIWS Gatling gun that can fire up to four thousand 20mm rounds per minute. Initially, the projectile consisted of depleted uranium, and later the round was made of titanium. The idea was to fire a round that was of the highest density and would not shatter upon impact. Titanium was slightly better than uranium, and could penetrate the armor of most small to medium ships, and aircraft were easy targets. After modernization, each ship of the *Iowa* class had four of these guns, which, in combination, had excellent coverage of 360 degrees around the ship. *Author's Collection*

did not matter that the ships cost very little to maintain. Finally, after being confronted with overwhelming facts and an absolute need to counter the *Kirov* class, the anti-battleship faction was convinced to at least silence its opinion. The need to checkmate the Soviets and the thought of a blue-water nuclear-powered surface ship with long-range missiles threatening American carriers and troop-laden amphibious groups persuaded a doubtful Congress that the battleships were needed.

Considering that it would take at least five to seven years and a multibillion-dollar price tag to design and build a ship to match the *Kirov*, refurbishing the *Iowa*

class made economic sense. The cost-cutters and annoying accountants became diehard *Iowa*-class proponents.

Even if new ships could have been built, they would not have had the 18-inch-thick, tempered-steel armor that could withstand most of the punishment that could be dealt by a *Kirov*. And the Tomahawk and Harpoon missiles were potent weapons that placed the *Iowa*s on a par with any warships that the Soviet navy could put to sea.

Refurbishing ships built four decades earlier with a design that was a half-century old sounded insane, yet there was no alternative that could be brought to bear quickly and effectively. The *Iowa* class, although against all conventional wisdom, was the choice of wisdom. After all, rifles have been in use for five hundred years with little real modifications, yet they still are of value.

There was no secret about the *Iowa* class being brought out of retirement. The Soviet navy was stunned by this development; it knew that the *Kirov*'s new adversary would be extremely dangerous and could easily thwart its tactical planning. In addition, the Soviet navy was having some rather serious problems with the *Kirov* class: one of the ships had reactor difficulties, and another had problems with the hull cracking at crucial locations.

The *Iowa*s were a well-founded class built during World War II and properly maintained during the interim periods. Each time they were decommissioned, the crews worked diligently to ensure that the ships were properly oiled, greased, painted, and made ready for the next recommissioning. (This diligence was somewhat true of all ships of all classes put into mothballs and a hallmark of the entire program. If mothballed ships could not be readied for combat within one to three months, then the program was valueless.) In fact, periodic detailed surveys of the *Iowa* class reported that they were in excellent condition and had many years of serviceable life remaining.

These surveys and the navy's overall reluctance to scrap the *Iowa* class kept the ships from being broken up, a good thing for the nation. Their new assignment was to destroy surface ships that threatened allied troop convoys, carrier battle groups, and any other surface groups. The battleships were also still ideal for pinpoint accuracy in shore bombardment. They could deliver firepower to an area in a few minutes that would take aircraft an entire day, at the risk of losing pilots to antiaircraft fire.

The USS *Iowa* (BB-61) just two weeks prior to its third commissioning. She is the epitome of old and new, and more than a match for the *Kirov* class of nuclear-assisted battle cruiser. The *Iowa* was recommissioned on September 23, 1983, and then began its part in the Cold War that lasted until 1991. *U.S. Navy*

MODERNIZATION AND OVERHAUL

The first *Iowa*-class ship to enter dry dock and begin the modernization process was the *New Jersey*. The battleship began the rehabilitation by leaving the Inactive Fleet Maintenance Facility, also called the Reserve Fleet anchorage, in Bremerton, Washington, for its old home, Long Beach, California. The *New Jersey* then spent the better part of the very early 1980s in the yard being modernized. The original cost for the *New Jersey* in the early 1940s was $100 million, and the 1980s upgrade was $496 million. Much of the preliminary work had already been done during the workup for the Vietnam War in the late 1960s, so the required modernization was not nearly as comprehensive. When the ship left the Long Beach yard and was recommissioned on December 28, 1982, she was definitely a battleship, yet there were obvious additions and changes.

A helicopter helipad had already replaced the twin catapults and the 40mm quad Bofors antiaircraft guns aft. Armored box launchers (ABL) for the BGM-109 series Tomahawk cruise missiles were evident amidships, as were eight RGM-84 Harpoon antiship missiles in two Mark 141 Kevlar-armored canisters amidships. The armored boxes were used extensively as aftermarket additions on the four recommissioned battleships and several of the nuclear and other commissioned cruisers. (Ultimately, the armored boxes for the Tomahawk missiles and canisters for the Harpoon missiles would give way to the vertical launch system (VLS), which was built into a ship's hull. The missiles, too, would be drastically improved, and by 2006, new generations were far more capable than those installed aboard the *Iowa* class in the 1980s.)

The *New Jersey* also was armed with four Gatling-gun-like weapons called the Mark 15 Phalanx CIWS. These had 20mm M61 Vulcan guns that were radar directed and could literally destroy an incoming shell. The guns could fire up to 3,000 rounds of depleted uranium (a very heavy and dense metal now replaced by titanium) per minute. The Mark 15 allowed for full 360-degree target coverage on an automated basis and had an effective range of 2,000 yards. The shell path could actually saw a ship in half with its firepower.

All of the older 40mm Bofors and 20mm Oerlikon guns had been removed by this time. At the height of the kamikaze scare in the final year of World War II, each of the *Iowa*-class battleships had twenty 5-inch guns and up to seventy-six 40mm and fifty-two 20mm guns pointed skyward to fight off the suicide pilots. The targets were swarms of aircraft of most remaining types in the Japanese military aircraft inventory, which, flying at up to 400 knots per hour, would select a large ship and dive on it. As a consequence, not only was every vacant space on the battleship's deck crowded with antiaircraft guns, but all Allied ships in the danger zone around the Philippines and Okinawa were also overarmed with anti-kamikaze weapons. It was estimated that a minimum of 24,000 shells had to be fired by defending ships to shoot down one determined kamikaze! With enough metal in the air, most of the attacking suicide planes were knocked down, but many broke through and either damaged or sunk nearly 240 Allied ships.

With the advent of jet propulsion, aircraft with speeds over 500 knots required a quicker-reacting weapon that could fire a hoselike pattern of shells more than one mile with accuracy unheard of in 1945. An

The armored conning tower which is a hallmark of almost all modern U.S. Navy battleships, and especially the fast battleships of the mid-twentieth century. Inside is the control and communication center for the ship, and the captain can look out through armored slits in the tower. *Author's Collection*

old-fashioned, Civil War–type Gatling Gun with a late-twentieth-century twist was needed, so the radar-weapon-integrated Vulcan CIWS was born to combat high-speed attack jets, missiles, and even medium-caliber shells. The rebuilt *Iowa* class had four Phalanx

CIWS units sited two per side, amidships and high up on the superstructure in order to cover every vantage point of the ship. (Since the 1980s, the CIWS has gone through a number of upgrades, and now the Mark 15 Block 1B adds a surface tracker to engage high-speed maneuvering targets as well as modern missiles.)

HEAVY WEAPONS: MISSILES AND GUNS

Aside from the close-in weapons systems, the *Iowa* class was rearmed with the RGM-84 Harpoon long-range antiship missile and some of the early models of BGM-109

The interior of the armored conning tower aboard the USS *Missouri* is the same as that aboard the *Iowa*. The vision slits can be seen as well as the steering wheel for the ship and engine controls. The bulkhead has the telephones to communicate with other compartments aboard the ship. *Author's Collection*

The modernized USS *Iowa* was photographed on April 24, 1984, the day before its recommissioning, at the Ingalls Shipbuilding Company, a division of Litton Corporation, in Pascagoula, Mississippi. *U.S. Navy*

Tomahawk cruise missile. The Harpoon has a maximum range of 64 or 85 nautical miles and can be armed with a 510-pound high-explosive warhead. The Tomahawk can carry a nuclear land-attack warhead up to 758 nautical miles, and its BGM -109C land-attack variant has a range of 2,643 nautical miles. The Tomahawk could fly at 760 miles per hour and had three configurations: antiship with a 250-nautical-mile range, land attack with a small nuclear warhead and a range of 1,500 nautical miles, and land attack with a 1,000-pound conventional warhead at a range of 700 nautical miles. Moreover, the Tomahawk could hit the target with 80 percent certainty. Both the Tomahawk and Harpoon are guided by either radar or, in the case of certain Tomahawk variants, terrain contour matching.

These over-the-horizon weapons are fairly accurate and quite deadly. (The concept of an arsenal ship loaded with over five hundred missile silos emerged from the *Iowa* class's modernization, yet has not become anywhere near reality.)

The *Iowa* and her sisters had the main and secondary batteries they were originally built with—nine 16-inch 50-caliber guns in the three turrets (two forward and one aft) and the twin-mount 5-inch 38-caliber guns. Originally, the *Iowa* class had twenty of the 5-inch weapons, but this number was shorn to twelve barrels in three turrets per side, due to the need for space and weight considerations.

The 16-inch guns could lob either a 2,700-pound armor-piercing shell over 24 miles or a 1,900-pound

The reason for the *Iowa* and its three sisters. The *Iowa* lets go with a full broadside to starboard. The *Iowa*-class battleships were indeed beautiful warships, and even with the 1980s modernization, they retained their aesthetic beauty. *U.S. Navy*

high-explosive (HE) shell the same distance. The armor-piercing shell could penetrate up to 22 inches of armor, depending on the angle at which the shell hit the target. Among the 16-inch shells available, there were twelve distinct projectile types for different purposes. Even with analog computers and what we would term old-fashioned fire control, the accuracy was phenomenal. The destructive power was amazing, and viewing all nine shells of a broadside in flight from an *Iowa*-class battleship was a rare treat, captured on film on few occasions.

As to the 5-inch weapons, there were ten types available, ranging from high-capacity to illumination, or star, shells. The maximum range was 18,200 yards for the 55.1-pound shell.

The weapons were not the sole defenses for the *Iowa* class. The ships were now equipped with electronic counter measures (ECM) and threat-warning systems that were designed to electronically counter enemy radar, missile-guidance systems, and other targeting devices. The ECM were concentrated in at least two AN/SLQ 32V antennas and installed aboard most ships, including fast combat-support ships, all surface combatants, and amphibious assault craft. The ECM were designed to confuse enemy threats, deceive incoming missile-guidance radars, and jam other radar types.

Aside from the electronic defenses, the *Iowa* class was the most survivable of ships in the world, with its armor protection and hundreds of watertight compartments. In addition, the ships were tributes to modern damage control; they could withstand immense punishment and keep fighting. The combination of a modern battleship with super-modern electronics created a virtual King Kong of the sea, and the marriage of these elements made for a highly formidable offensive and defensive weapon.

Had a *Kirov* battle cruiser ever challenged an *Iowa*-class battleship, the *Kirov* would have been shattered in the first volley of weapons.

An *Iowa*-class battleship lets go with its 16-inch main battery. There is nothing quite as awesome as the sensation of a full broadside of these weapons. Using the 2,700-pound ammunition, the Iowa could throw 24,300 pounds, or 12.3 tons, of destructive force some 27 land miles. Even though the ships employed analog computers, the accuracy was remarkable. *Author's Collection*

CHAPTER NINE

TRAGEDY STRIKES THE *IOWA*

The USS *Iowa*, with its three sisters, was considered the finest heavy warship ever built for any navy in the world. This was true in 1944, and in the late 1980s its superiority was even more evident. At nearly 60,000 tons, these battleships had been upgraded to a level commensurate with naval warfare needs of the 1980s and up through the end of the century.

These ships now had state-of-the-art surface-to-surface Harpoon missiles and could defeat any threat that the Soviet navy or any Soviet bloc navy could put to sea. The objective of the U.S. Navy to counter the Soviet Navy's *Kirov* class nuclear battle cruiser had been achieved, and there had been no need to build an expensive from-the-keel-up warship to accomplish the same end.

The *Iowa* participated in a number of high-profile operations in the Atlantic, Indian Ocean, Mediterranean, and Persian Gulf during the late 1980s. The presence of a battleship leading a surface-action group kept Soviet naval units and ambitions at bay. In early December 1987, the *Iowa* arrived in Diego Garcia, a lonely American outpost in the Indian Ocean. The purpose was to make a show of maximum force in the areas leading to the northern Arabian Gulf and through the Strait of Hormuz. Escorting unarmed oil tankers and other ships in convoy to their destinations was of immense value to the world's energy supply. Insurgents, fanatics, and other politically driven groups had sent high-speed boats armed with missiles and heavy machine guns to intercept and interfere with the world's oil delivery routes. Sinking even one supertanker could change world oil prices and cause great difficulty within high-oil-use nations. A battleship-led surface-action group could ensure that the amateur attackers could be kept at their moorings or destroyed before they could interdict any convoys. The specter of the 16-inch guns firing caused unimaginable fear in potential attackers.

After the *Iowa*'s primary operation was completed in the Near East, she returned to the United States and her home port of Norfolk. After a period of overhaul and repair in dry dock, the battleship steamed for the firing range at Vieques Island, Puerto Rico. On January 26, 1989, the *Iowa* fired the longest-range shell in history at the island target. This shot from a Mark-7 16-inch 50-caliber gun set an unbroken record in distance. It traveled 23.4

The USS *Missouri* (BB-11), clearly an older version than the *Missouri* of World War II and beyond fame. Commissioned on December 1, 1903, it is seen in this photo during World War I. On April 3, 1904, the aft turret experienced a flareback that instantly killed thirty-six men. It was not unlike that which occurred aboard the USS *Iowa* eighty-five years later. *U.S. Navy*

nautical miles (26.9 land miles) and accurately hit the designated target.

THE MARK-7 16-INCH 50-CALIBER GUN

Despite the electronic and weapons upgrades of the 1980s, it was the nine Mark-7 16-inch 50-caliber guns designed decades before most of the crew was born that defined the *Iowa*-class battleship. The comment was always, "Yes I know it has missiles and nuclear weapons, but just look at those huge guns." The big guns have always impressed the lay persons. The *Iowa* class had three turrets with three barrels each, and could fire up to two rounds per barrel per minute. Some of the battleships had even achieved a short-duration rate of one salvo every fifty seconds. The average barrel had a lifetime of 290 rounds before requiring a relining. This number may sound sizeable, but when a battleship was called upon for shore bombardment and perhaps a big-gun duel with other capital ships, it didn't take long to fire that many rounds. The *Iowa* fired a grand total of

11,834 rounds between 1943 and November 20, 1989, and had fired 2,873 shells during its final commission (1984–1989).

As to the powder charges that impelled the shells, there were approximately fifty thousand silken bags, each weighing about 110 pounds, used throughout the *Iowa*'s career. After World War II, the powder charge or propellant was made up of a cooler-burning substance that prolonged barrel-lining endurance. Six 110-pound bags of propellant was the maximum that could be rammed up against a shell. In actuality, the bags were not filled with powder, but with pellets, which were far safer in the confines of the turret and the loading mechanism and more effective. Although the bags were rugged and reasonably safe, they were still treated with respect by crews who feared an explosion or flareback.

The Mark-7 16-inch 50-caliber gun could fire a variety of projectiles, such as the 1,900-pound service shell, a 1,900-pound high-capacity shell, and 2,700-pound target or armor-piercing shell. The 2,700-pound shell with a 660-pound charge had an optimum range of 42,345 yards at an elevation of 45 degrees. This translated to a range of 24.06 land miles or 23.24 nautical miles. In theory and under optimum conditions, the battleships in the *Iowa* class could fire up to eighteen rounds or projectiles per minute. Although this rate did not have the smothering effect of the 6-inch 47-caliber weapons in the main battery of certain American light cruisers, which could fire 180 rounds per minute, it was a respectable amount of highly destructive firepower.

The *Iowa*-class battleships had participated in a number of operations from World War II through the Cold War. This experience, plus the knowledge gained from other classes of battleships with 16-inch weapons, resulted in refined training and procedures for accurate, safe, and consistently expeditious firing of the main battery.

Unfortunately, after the *Iowa* class was brought out of retirement in the 1980s, the main battery was nearly a half-century old. There were a few gunners remaining in the navy who had seen service on the sole *Iowa*-class battleship deployed to Vietnam, the USS *New Jersey* (BB-62) in 1969, but the vast majority of naval personnel who had originally perfected their skill with this weapon were no longer available. It fell to new officers and men to learn an old trade. As proof of a difficult learning curve that faced the new main-battery staff, the USS *New Jersey* fired a number of rounds against Syrian artillery emplacements in Beirut in 1982 with dismal results, especially in shell placement on target. There was serious concern about this and other difficulties that seemed to emerge with operating the huge weapon. After all, its design had come from the immediate post–World War I era, long before most of the navy's gunnery ratings and

officers had been born. The navy needed a training program that was more formal than on-the-job training with decades-old manuals and that did not depend on the declining memories of men who fired these guns during the Vietnam War. So the navy sought outside assistance. RCA signed a contract to develop a thirty-six- to forty-two-week course in the operation of this weapon, with emphasis on safety and getting the most out of this throwback to another age. It was up to each ship's captain to ensure that safety predominated, as it was becoming clear that a surface engagement with the Soviet navy was only marginally possible.

In the years leading up to the collapse of the Soviet Union in early 1990 and the Persian Gulf War, the four *Iowa*-class battleships, as lead elements in surface-action groups, performed magnificently and were deemed a successful program even by their most ardent detractors. But the battleships' opponents had been waiting for any failure in this program—especially with the use of the nine 16-inch 50-caliber guns as well as the twelve 5-inch 38-caliber guns in the secondary battery—to justify retiring these four ships as soon as possible. Modernists felt that any expenditure on defense weaponry had to be on weapons of the future and not those of the past.

Gun or turret explosions were not uncommon on U.S. warships. As far back as February 29, 1844, the USS *Princeton*, the U.S. Navy's first screw-propelled warship, fired one of its new wrought-iron 12-inch guns, dubbed the Peacemaker. It had been fired several times on the day before, and against the strong advice of the *Princeton*'s officers, the experimental gun was again fired. This time it exploded and killed the secretary of the navy, secretary of state, and four other

The battleship USS *Mississippi* (BB-41) during the 1920s. Over a period of twenty years, this ship had two flarebacks in the center barrel of Turret No. 2. In total, the death toll was ninety-one men. The *Mississippi* investigations determined that the cause was the same as for most flarebacks—over-ramming and powder breaking out of the silken bags. *Author's Collection*

prominent political or naval officers, as well as wounding twenty other guests.

The early-twentieth-century battleship USS *Missouri* (BB-11) attempted to fire one of its 12-inch guns in its aft twin-barrel turret on April 13, 1904, during target practice off the Virginia Capes. The ship had been engaged in target practice most of the day, and suddenly a flareback in the port gun ignited its powder charge and then the next two charges in line. A flareback is akin to accidentally lighting a complete box of matches. All of the surrounding oxygen is consumed and the heat is beyond control, yet only for a short period. The next phase is acrid, toxic smoke. No human can survive it. Thirty-six men in the turret were killed instantly due to suffocation, yet the ship was not vaporized by a massive explosion. Men on deck and below rushed to assist their shipmates, and the bravery displayed resulted in three Medals of Honor being awarded for heroism.

A nearly identical flareback occurred aboard the battleship USS *Mississippi* (BB-41) on June 12, 1924, and again during wartime on November 20, 1943. Like the *Missouri* before and the USS *Iowa* to follow, the gun crews were instantly killed: forty-eight men in 1924 and forty-three men in 1943. One macabre story tells how as the dead were being removed at the *Mississippi's* base

in San Pedro, California, in 1924, a swaying hand of one of the corpses accidentally struck the firing switch, and the port barrel fired. Its shell landed harmlessly in the bay. However, it terrified even the most grizzled boatswain's mate!

The turret explosion on the *Mississippi* in 1943 occurred during the bombardment of the Gilbert Islands. Due to the importance of that invasion, known as Operation Galvanic, the *Mississippi*, in true navy tradition, continued firing on targets after the explosion, using her remaining three main battery turrets. When the dependent and grateful marines felt the *Mississippi* and her highly accurate main battery were no longer needed, the ship was freed to seek repair.

On a related issue, the USS *South Dakota* (BB-57) experienced a severe explosion of a high-capacity powder in a tank (a metal container in which propellant charges are stored) in Turret No. 2, which in turn ignited four other powder tanks. The *South Dakota* was in the process of taking on ammunition from the USS *Wrangell* (AE-12), an ammunition ship off Okinawa on May 6, 1945. Three men from the *South Dakota* were killed instantly, eight later died of injuries, and twenty-four other gunnery staff suffered injuries. The damage would have been greater if the Turret No. 2 magazines

A line drawing of the USS *South Dakota* (BB-57). This particular battleship, which was a great nemesis to attacking Japanese aircraft, suffered explosions in Turret No. 2 on May 6, 1945, while taking on ammunition from the USS *Wrangell* (AE-12). Had the explosions gone further, the ship might have ceased to exist. *U.S. Navy*

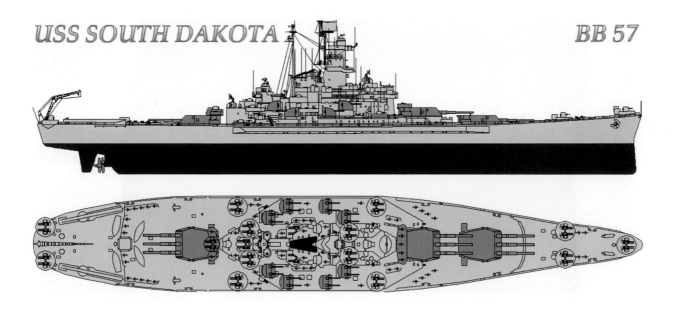

USS SOUTH DAKOTA   BB 57

The USS *Wrangell* (AE-12), an 11,295-ton ammunition ship that served in World War II, was recommissioned during the Korean Conflict and continued into the Vietnam War. Eventually, the ship was disposed of by the U.S. Maritime Administration (MARAD) on November 1, 1986. Had the *South Dakota* exploded in May 1945, the *Wrangell* would have been severely damaged if not sunk. *U.S. Navy*

had not been flooded. The tempo of the war was hot, and by July 1, 1945, the battleship was repaired and back on line.

Battleships were not the only class of warship to experience this type of tragedy. In 1952, the *Baltimore*-class heavy cruiser USS *Saint Paul* (CA-73) lost thirty men in Turret No. 2 as the result of a fire. The ship had been bombarding North Korean targets and ports, and a cartridge (not a powder charge) contributed to the rapidly burning fire and toxic fumes.

Twenty years later, in the very early hours of October 1, 1972, a defective 8-inch shell detonated in the center barrel of Turret No. 2 aboard the heavy cruiser USS *Newport News* (CA-148). The cruiser was lying off

the coast of Vietnam providing gunfire support to forces ashore. The powder charge first flared and caused the shell to explode. Within seconds, two other powder cartridges in the powder/shell train also burned, and the result was twenty men killed and thirty-six seriously injured. Acrid smoke filled the forward part of the ship and killed three of the twenty. The explosive force was so great that it blew the gun barrel out of the turret, and only the barrel liner held it precariously in place. As with most other ships that experience a flareback, there was little major damage to the interior of the turret, the other seventeen men were instantaneously killed from suffocation and toxic smoke.

The USS *St. Paul* (CA-73), a heavy cruiser armed with nine 8-inch 55-caliber guns, and twelve 5-inch 38-caliber guns in the secondary battery. On April 21, 1952, thirty personnel died in Turret No. 2 of the main battery while firing on North Korean targets. Later the ship was used in the film, *In Harm's Way*, starring John Wayne and directed by Otto Preminger. *U.S. Navy*.

The heavy cruiser USS *Newport News* (CA-148), with its tubular-type mast, almost looks like a pocket battleship. At 0110 hours on October 1, 1972, the *Newport News* was called upon to fire on enemy targets in Vietnam. Unfortunately, an 8-inch shell prematurely exploded in the center barrel of Turret No. 2. This in turn ignited shells in the hoist leading to the loading tray, and a flareback was added to a confined detonation. Twenty of the gun crew were instantly killed. Again, the magazine was closed, and thus any explosive residue or fire was prevented from spreading to shells that could have blown the forward half of the ship off. *U.S. Navy*

If similar accidents were to happen aboard any of the modernized *Iowa*-class ships, then many in Washington, D.C., power positions would again be forced to admit the continued value of the battleship in the microchip and cruise-missile era. Unfortunately, a tragedy on the USS *Iowa* on April 19, 1989, provided the impetus for mothballing the battleships again.

FLAREBACK ABOARD THE USS *IOWA*

In the American naval service, everything humanly possible is done to prevent shipboard accidents, because personnel can be and often are killed or maimed. Plus, millions of dollars in taxpayer property can be destroyed and the ship can be taken out of service. Many accidents result in major disasters. Mistakes are due to large numbers of men with varying degrees of training and skill

operating massive warships with complicated and interrelated systems. Most accidents are due to human error, and it is rare that sabotage or fits of emotional behavior lead to accidents. The cause of most accidents can ultimately be determined, yet explosions or flarebacks in turrets are extremely difficult to trace to any but the most obvious origin: accidental exposure of powder or shell contents to massive heat. A few accidents go wholly unexplained.

On April 19, 1989, the USS *Iowa* was engaged in some vital target practice to determine if it was possible to accurately and safely fire a projectile beyond twenty-four nautical miles. Suddenly, a flareback occurred in Turret No. 2. It rapidly consumed twenty-five of forty-five bags of propellant stored on the deck of the powder flat (the storage area for powder bags) plus three that

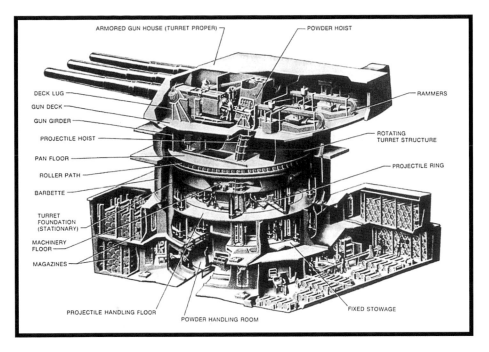

ARMORED GUN HOUSE (TURRET PROPER)
POWDER HOIST
DECK LUG
GUN DECK
GUN GIRDER
PROJECTILE HOIST
PAN FLOOR
ROLLER PATH
BARBETTE
TURRET FOUNDATION (STATIONARY)
MACHINERY FLOOR
MAGAZINES
RAMMERS
ROTATING TURRET STRUCTURE
PROJECTILE RING
PROJECTILE HANDLING FLOOR
POWDER HANDLING ROOM
FIXED STOWAGE

A cutaway of a typical 16-inch turret and handling rooms, as well as its magazine in an *Iowa*-class battleship. This was produced by the U.S. Navy as a training aid. Every possible safety plan and procedure has been brought to play. It was recognized that spending years to build a battleship could be erased by one careless move, and the navy did not want that to happen. *U.S. Navy*

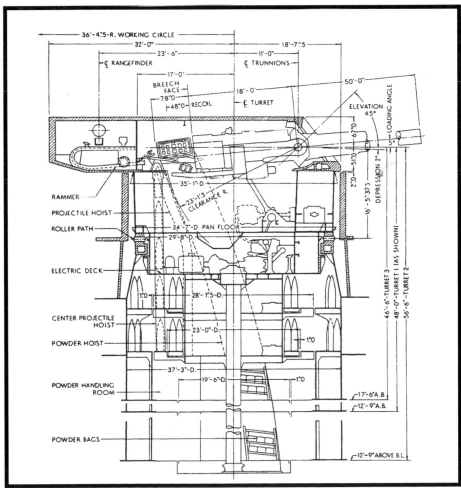

A cutaway drawing of a 16-inch gun graphically depicts the path that shell and powder bags take on their way to being fired at the enemy. The key is to keep powder and shells moving toward the gun that is to be fired, yet never stack them if a holdup occurs in the powder and shell line. A second major issue is to ensure that if any danger does present itself—the train is stopped to prevent too many shells and powder from entering the turret. *U.S. Navy*

The emergency hatchway under a main-battery turret of the *Missouri*. Crawling into or out of the turret almost requires contortionist skills. A hard hat is a must for any visitor, or a bump on the head is probable. However, this hatch must be closed and locked during firing. The hatch under the *Iowa* is currently welded shut to keep intruders out from where the forty-seven crewmen were killed. *Author's Collection*

had been loaded in the center gun. The intense heat and consumption of oxygen, combined with toxic gases, fumes, and smoke, resulted in the immediate death of forty-seven officers and men.

After a serious accident occurs, an exhaustive study of forensics, survivor testimony, and intelligent analysis are used to determine the cause. The scene of an accident of this proportion is always treated akin to a crime scene, so that the investigators have as much evidence to work with as possible. Unfortunately, the *Iowa's* Turret No. 2 was cleaned and repainted before the ship returned to port, and the former crew attested to the fact that residue from the flareback was hosed over the side of the ship immediately after the tragedy. By the time the *Iowa* reached Puerto Rico Naval Station (Roosevelt Roads) to discharge the forty-seven bodies, the accident scene had been completely cleaned and thus contaminated, making any proper investigation by experts nearly impossible.

The U.S. Navy's initial investigation proposed some

This is a photo of the interior of the main battery gun room on an *Iowa*-class battleship. The actual turret is heavily protected by armor, which includes 17 inches on the faceplate, 9.5 inches on the sides, 12 inches on the back side, and 7.25 inches on the roof. Only the armored conning tower at 17.5 inches thickness and the barbette (under the turret) to the second deck at 17.3 inches are greater. *U.S. Navy*

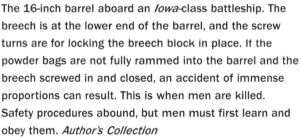

The 16-inch barrel aboard an *Iowa*-class battleship. The breech is at the lower end of the barrel, and the screw turns are for locking the breech block in place. If the powder bags are not fully rammed into the barrel and the breech screwed in and closed, an accident of immense proportions can result. This is when men are killed. Safety procedures abound, but men must first learn and obey them. *Author's Collection*

Another view of the breech and the breech block. Below the breech is another compartment, which is the shell handling room. A tray can be lowered to transfer powder bags and the shells, 1,900-pound high-capacity (HC) or 2,700-pound armor piercing (AP), from storage areas and into the barrel. The tray, shown here in its up position, is then withdrawn. The entire process of bringing up a shell and five or six powder bags—placing them on the tray— ramming them into the barrel, and firing all must take thirty seconds or less. This is why training and repetitive drills are vital for safety and getting the job done. *Author's Collection*

very lurid causes for the explosion. There were charges of a homosexual love affair between the acting center-gun captain, Gunner's Mate 2nd Clayton Hartwig, and another sailor. Hartwig was accused of placing an incendiary device in the loading tray or between the powder bags, which produced the heat to ignite the bags prematurely. This allegation was based on the presence of some household chemicals that could cause a detonation. The ship's captain and presiding senior officer of the preliminary investigation, Rear Admiral Richard Milligan, said Hartwig was likely guilty. Hartwig's motives, Milligan said, were suicidal feelings over a love affair that had

gone wrong and the desire to collect on a large insurance policy he had taken out on his own life. Regrettably, there were few real facts and a great deal of supposition in the accusations against Hartwig.

When these findings were published in September 1989, many in the U.S. Congress were outraged by this outlandish reason given for the accident. Milligan's report was discounted as a personal attack on one

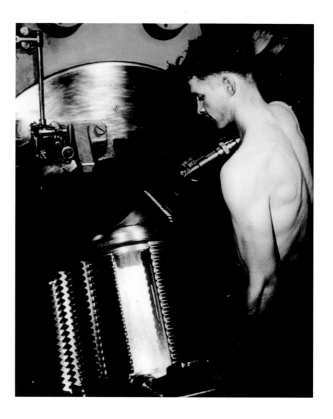

On the morning of December 14, 1986, Captain Larry Seaquist and the gunnery staff for Turret No. 2 selected a 1,900-pound high-capacity (HC) round with a Mark 29 PDF, or primary direction of fire, for firing from the starboard barrel. This projectile is special to the ship and its crew, as it is the one thousandth shell successfully fired since the USS *Iowa* was recommissioned. The gunner's mate with an asbestos glove to prevent being burned is watching the shell emerging from the magazine on the shell hoist before being transferred to the spanning tray. It will be rammed into the barrel prior to a reduced powder charge of 305 pounds of D840 SPDN propellant, the firing keys will be closed in another compartment, and the shell will be safely on its way. *U.S. Navy*

A gunner's mate shuts the breech door of the 16-inch 50-caliber gun barrel after ensuring that everything is true and correct. The shell and the proper number of bags are in the breech before this individual can shut the heavy breech block, which turns to screw-lock itself in place. *U.S. Navy*

A second investigation tested as many variables as was reasonably possible, but little changed in the determination and still did not discount the possibility of sabotage by Hartwig. This second report was also suspect. The truth lay somewhere else. Demands for renewed and independent investigations were called for.

A further investigation provided the following information and conclusions.

On the morning of April 19, the ship was operating in the Caribbean on an exercise dubbed FLEETEX 3-89. This exercise involved the test firing of its main battery with a variety of powder charges. After Turret No. 1 had fired and experienced a misfire in the left barrel, Turret No. 2 began its loading and firing sequence upon instructions from the bridge. All three barrels were to be loaded with dummy shells. A five-bag special charge of D846 propellant was selected, and although the use of this type of propellant in this environment was unusual, it was still

individual and a witch hunt for a saboteur. Many in Congress, including Senator Sam Nunn of the Senate Armed Services Committee, were highly skeptical of the findings, as was the press. Many in the public complained that this report was self-serving and the conclusions absurd. It disregarded the ancient ammunition, outdated ship technology, and poor crew training. The U.S. Navy was embarrassed by the shoddy preliminary investigation, and ultimately, the findings were proven to be linked more to homophobia than reality.

On April 19, 1989, in the Caribbean, the USS *Iowa* accidentally experiences a flareback in its center barrel in Turret No. 2. This is the first actual photograph of a flareback as taken from the bridge. The numbers 1 and 3 barrels are in their firing positions, whereas number 2 is in its optimal loading position. The bloomers have been blown off the guns, and smoke and acrid chemical fumes are forcibly coming out of every aperture in the turret. All life in the turret is now gone, and the loss of these men does not in any way resemble a film or movie as produced by Hollywood. *Author's Collection*

regarded as safe. The maximum pressure with this charge was in the 39,000 psi range, which was substantially lower than the normal pressure of 49,700 psi, and well within the 90,000 psi maximum in the barrel mechanism.

Within forty-four seconds of the command to load, barrels 1 and 2 were loaded and ready. Barrel 2 (center) had been loaded with its projectile, and next came powder bags 1 and 2, which would be followed up by three more bags, all rammed in at a slow speed. Hartwig was the acting gun captain of barrel 2. The turret captain, Senior Chief Gunner's Mate Reginald Ziegler, complimented the crew for its loading of the left barrel and then said, "Center gun is having a little trouble. We'll straighten that out."

The bridge was listening to the conversation and anxious for all guns to be loaded and ready to fire. Within seconds, Richard Lawrence, the center gun cradleman, said, "I have a problem here; I am not ready yet." Ziegler said to Lieutenant Junior Grade Robert Buch, "Tell plot we are not ready yet. There is a problem in the center gun!" Not long after this exchange, Lawrence again, with exasperation and some fear, complained, "I am not ready yet! I am not ready yet!"

The next and last voice from Turret No. 2 simply uttered, "Oh my. . . ."

The breech to the center gun had not been closed, and the projectile and a number of powder bags were exposed. A huge fireball then swept through the entire turret and erupted through the gun bloomers, the black, heavy canvas covers that were attached to the barrels outside the turret. The bloomers were ripped loose from all of the barrels and blown away from the turret. The interior of the turret was consumed by the flareback, and forty-seven men were killed outright. The fire did not spread to the magazine; if it had, an explosion, rivaled only by that of the HMS *Hood* after being hit by the German battleship *Bismarck*, would have vaporized the entire ship. Antiflash seals in the scuttles to the powder magazine saved the ship and the eleven crewmen down below the rotating turret system.

The heat generated was intense, and hot gases escaping from the turret burned the adjoining teak deck. An order to flood the magazine quickly ended any further possibility of explosion, yet it took over ninety minutes to extinguish all of the fires.

What had caused this to occur?

Further analysis was carried out at the Sandia National Laboratories in conjunction with the navy. The tests were more forensic and less humanistic in nature. The result was a more plausible assessment of what truly happened in Turret No. 2 than previous investigations presented.

The tests found that the explosive pellets (tubular nitrocellulose) in the silk powder bag trim layer could have been too few in this particular bag. An examination of a random sample of pellet bags aboard the *Iowa* determined that the bags had a range of one to sixty-five pellets in the trim layer. The fewer the pellets, the greater the opportunity for a flareback in an over-ram situation. If the mechanical bag rammer was set on fast rather than slow speed as required for five bags, then it was possible that a pre-ignition could have taken place before the breech was closed.

The best scientific minds from Sandia testified before Congress on May 25, 1990, that they could not completely ignore the possibility of a foreign object being employed to pre-ignite the propellant bags; however,

Red-helmeted damage-control men fight the fire in Turret No. 2 and wash the debris over the side. Unfortunately, some of the debris included human parts from the forty-seven men in the turret. *Author's Collection*

Water was continually played onto the turret to prevent any further damage, and to allow rescue teams to enter the turret to see if any of the crew was alive. The turret was cleaned and painted, and all of the remains of the dead were removed, yet the turret itself was to be left in the position where the barrels were pointed to the starboard (as shown) and the center barrel lowered as it was when the accident occurred. *U.S. Navy*

The dead from the *Iowa* are given a proper military funeral. Here they are brought home from Roosevelt Roads Naval Station to the ship's homeport of Norfolk, Virginia.
Author's Collection

The *Iowa* slowly and silently pulls into port at the Norfolk Navy Yard four days after the flareback that took the lives of forty-seven men in turret two. The three barrels of turret two overhang the pier where the media is grasping for every possible detail. The center barrel is in the exact position as when the flareback occurred, and the seamen and marines are standing at attention with black armbands. The ship's marine detachment surrounds the turret and is especially well turned out, and rock hard at attention. *U.S. Navy*

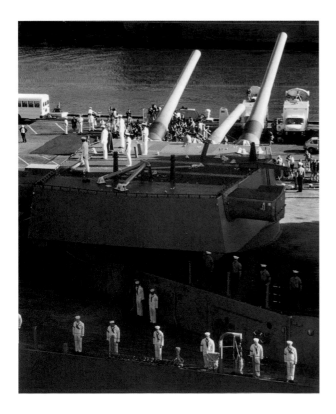

President and Mrs. Bush attend a memorial service for the forty-seven men who died in the turret accident. President Bush had been a U.S. Navy torpedo plane pilot in World War II in the Pacific and has mentioned his special affinity for navy people. *Author's Collection*

An *Iowa*-class battleship opens fire with its forward battery. This was not unlike the swan song of the *Iowa*. On the battleship's final journey back from its deployment in the Mediterranean in 1990, it fired its very last 16-inch shell, which was just under the 12,000th round fired since the ship was originally commissioned on February 22, 1943. Much had happened in the last forty-seven years: microchips, missiles, TV dinners and TVs, Super-Bowls, the end of the Soviet Union, and thousands of other changes. *Author's Collection*

it was more likely that an over-ram had occurred on bags with a disproportionate number of pellets in the trim layer. This has become the most accepted explanation of the flareback.

The crew turnover, lack of training, inadequate experience, and a six-week period without any practice on the guns were human causes contributing to the accident. It was not all mechanical errors on the part of the crew; they had forgotten or ignored basic managerial procedures. Added to this was the recent appointment of a new captain from a modern anti-aircraft destroyer, the USS *Kidd* (DDG-993). It was well known that Captain Moosally favored the missile capability of the *Iowa* as opposed to its gunnery department. This prejudice lowered morale among the gunners substantially.

A degree of vanity on the part of the senior officers may have also exacerbated the pre-disaster situation. The *Iowa* already held the record for accurately firing a 16-inch shell farther than any other ship in the world to date. It had achieved this feat on January 26, 1989, at Vieques Island, when the main-battery gun crew had fired a 16-inch projectile twenty-four nautical miles, or 27.60 land miles, and accurately hit the designated target. Yet the senior officers were pressing for improved loading and firing times as well as greater range.

All taken together, it was a recipe for disaster, and forty-seven lives eventually paid the price.

THE LAST REPAIR AND DECOMMISSIONING
The USS *Iowa* arrived at the Norfolk Naval Shipyard

Iowa Point in Norfolk. This is a permanently maintained memorial to the forty-seven men who lost their lives in Turret No. 2.
Author's Collection

on April 22, 1989, just days after the flashback tragedy. Ammunition was offloaded in accordance with procedure dating back to World War II, and repairs began immediately. By May 30, the "Big Stick" was ready for sea again, and by June 7, 1989, it had reloaded ammunition at the Whiskey Anchorage in Hampton Roads. The *Iowa* then departed for Europe.

During what would be its final deployment as an active fleet unit, the *Iowa* traveled 30,983 nautical miles or 35,630 land miles. It visited fifteen major southern European ports, as well as several important cities on the African continent. During this historic voyage, the *Iowa* embarked with the commander of the Sixth Fleet and for just over three months was the flagship of the fleet. On November 17, 1989, the fleet commander departed the *Iowa* and returned to the USS *Belknap* (CG-26), the permanent flagship

of the commander of the Sixth Fleet. (Just fourteen years prior, the *Belknap* suffered the loss of six men in a collision with the USS *John F. Kennedy* (CV-67) on November 22, 1975. This ship was no stranger to tragedy.)

With the flag of the Sixth Fleet returned to the *Belknap*, the *Iowa* bid farewell and steamed for Norfolk through the Strait of Gibraltar. During the transit to Norfolk, the ship fired a 16-inch gun for the last time; this made 2,873 rounds fired since its recommissioning in 1984.

On December 7, 1989, the namesake of the *Iowa*-class battleships arrived in Norfolk. The ship began preparations for what would become its final decommissioning and moved to Philadelphia. On April 19, 1990, a permanent memorial plaque was dedicated to the forty-seven who died a year earlier. It was placed in Turret No. 2, and few have ever seen it.

The USS *Iowa* opens fire with its main battery of 16-inch rifles. This event took place after the massive rebuilding of the four *Iowa*-class battleships, which brought them into the microchip era. The gunnery drill pre-dated the terrible accident that occurred in Turret No. 2 in April 1989. After that time and to this date, the turret has never been repaired, and a lonely plaque marks the death of forty-seven innocent lives that were snuffed out in a flareback on April 19, 1989. The hatches are welded shut, and access is strictly limited. Captain Fred Moosally, who was the ship's commanding officer on April 19, 1989, had the turret cleaned and painted before the ship reached its first port. This violation of NCIS (Navy Criminal Investigation Service) procedure made a conclusive investigation nearly impossible. Any aspirations the captain had for flag rank disappeared. *U.S. Navy*

CHAPTER TEN

THE BATTLE FOR A USS *IOWA* MUSEUM

The USS *Iowa* was formally decommissioned on October 26, 1990, just months after the beginning of a major new crisis in the Middle East, the Iraqi invasion of Kuwait. Despite the investigations that exonerated the ammunition and 16-inch gun system aboard the USS *Iowa*, the ship was not selected for combat in the Persian Gulf War (1990–1991) primarily due to Turret No. 2 being out of action and locked in forward train. Although two *Iowa*-class battleships would participate in the ensuing war, the USS *Iowa* and *New Jersey* had fired their last wartime shots. Military, political, and economic realities were changing, and these battleships' days were numbered.

Naval enthusiasts' love for battleships is undeniable, and even when compared to today's ultramodern littoral combat ship, the battleships still triumph in the eyes of all who gaze upon them. Many in the leadership of the Department of the Navy, including those in the Marine Corps, are reluctant to let go of this last vestige of an era gone by until gunfire bombardment with a range of at least sixty-three miles is guaranteed to marines who are securing or holding a deep beachhead. This type of bombardment has become all but fully operational in the extended-range guided munitions (ERGM) that can be fired by the Mark 45, Model 4, 5-inch 62-caliber gun now being installed aboard the newer *Arleigh Burke*-class destroyers and retrofitted to several of the *Ticonderoga*-class Aegis missile cruisers. And there is the ever valuable Tomahawk cruise-missile variant that can be used for land-attack purposes. Since the 1990–1991 Persian Gulf War, there have been hundreds of Tomahawks fired at enemy targets, with constantly improved accuracy. This missile, in its various modes, has become the weapon of choice for theater and national commanders.

Yet even with these developments, the wheels of Congress have turned very slowly, and their slowness is only rivaled by that of the Pentagon. It was well known by any individual with a sense of the future that the battleship's day had finally passed into history. Maintaining them on active duty included supporting over six thousand ratings and officers aboard ships whose systems were ancient and generally non-transferable to other areas in the U.S. Navy. Maintaining these battleships was a poor use of limited resources; therefore, the battleships were inactivated. All the *Iowa*-class battleships were decommissioned by

The *Iowa* dresses ship while visiting Portsmouth, England, in 1989. During this "flag-showing" cruise, the ship ultimately visited several countries in the Baltic and North Atlantic. The battleship temporarily replaced the cruiser USS *Belknap* (CG-26) as the flagship of the Sixth Fleet, and after surrendering this privilege, began its transit back to Norfolk. On November 26, 1989, the ship fired one last 16-inch shell. This translated to 2,873 16-inch shells fired in the 1980s commissioning, and a total of 11,834 rounds since its original commissioning on February 22, 1943. *U.S. Navy*

March 31, 1992. The *Missouri* was the final ship to go into reserve. The four battleships were laid up as if they would be recalled on short notice. That notice has never come, and after years of inactivity, most are being placed on the donation block.

The *Missouri* was towed from Bremerton, Washington, to Pearl Harbor via Astoria, Oregon. The water in the Columbia River at Astoria killed a microorganism that would have harmed the ecology of Pearl Harbor. The *Missouri* arrived at its berth in Pearl Harbor, just

yards from the USS *Arizona* Memorial, on June 22, 1998. The *Missouri* had added a final luster to its already spectacular contribution to American history and naval lore. As a major seaborne unit in Operations Desert Shield and Desert Storm, the *Missouri* fired 759 16-inch shells at Iraqi targets with great accuracy. She also lit up the night sky with Tomahawk missile launchings that sped to their targets in Iraq. When the *Missouri* passed by Oahu's Diamond Head on its way into the channel leading to Ford Island, enthusiasm for the ship ran high.

The *Iowa* sitting in dry dock in the Philadelphia Naval Shipyard. A casual look indicates that the hull requires a complete sandblasting, primer, anti-fouling paint, and regular black and gray paint. The four propellers will no doubt need polishing. Without substantial underwater work, the *Iowa* could not be expected to make its flank speed of more than 33 knots. *U.S. Navy*

The cover of the program brochure of the decommissioning ceremonies of the USS *Iowa* (BB-61) on October 26, 1990. The men who served aboard this ship and the other three *Iowa*-class battleships were cast to the winds of naval service, and within a few short years, their battleship skills were degraded. *Author's Collection*

Thousands of volunteers began crawling all over the ship when it opened as a museum on January 29, 1999. To this day, the *Missouri* has a permanent roster of twenty-five hundred volunteers who are devoted and knowledgeable. The memorial has been a smashing success, seeing a half-million visitors per year and having a complementary and very aggressive public-relations outreach.

The USS *New Jersey* also left the Reserve Fleet at Bremerton, Washington, for a rather long tow to the Philadelphia Naval Shipyard behind the oceangoing tug *Sea Victory*. It arrived in November 1999 and became a museum at Home Port Alliance, Camden, New Jersey, on October 15, 2001.

The USS *Wisconsin* fought well in the Persian Gulf War. On February 6, 1991, she replaced the *Missouri* on the gun line and prepared to blast Iraqi targets. The

battleship had already launched twenty-four Tomahawk missiles at Iraqi targets. After firing a number of 16-inch shells at artillery positions in Kuwait and at Iraqi high-speed boats, the *Missouri* and the *Wisconsin* began to concentrate fire on Faylaka Island to assist in the ground offensive.

The USS *Wisconsin* was decommissioned on September 30, 1991. After a period alongside the *Iowa* in Newport, Rhode Island, she was moved on April 16, 2001, to the Nauticus Museum in Norfolk, Virginia, where she became the centerpiece. Since she was still U.S. Navy property, no fees or admission charges could be levied.

As of April 2006, the *Wisconsin* was still being carried as a category B mobilization asset, and much of its interior electronics are off limits to the public. Although these systems have been eclipsed by more modern and

The *Wisconsin* and the *Iowa* are rafted together in the backwaters of the Philadelphia Navy Yard. Both remained chained together until the mid 1990s. Ultimately, they would be retained on the Naval Vessel Register (NVR) and considered able to respond to national emergencies. The years 2006–2007 should end the "category B," mobilization status for both of the ships. By 2007, they will have been out of the technical loop for nearly two decades. Time, sun, and inclement weather are the enemies of ships held in reserve. *U.S. Navy*

lethal electronic equipment, they are still considered to be relatively secure. The same holds true for her sister ship, the USS *Iowa*. Protecting the electronic packages is vital in the event the nation needs these ships again. Estimates as to how much it would take for a private museum group to conform to U.S. Navy security requirements run as high as $10 million. Fortunately, the *Wisconsin*, as part of the Nauticus naval and maritime center, draws over five hundred thousand visitors per year, and that figure has remained static since the ship was open to the public. This drawing power translates into a steady increase in donations, sales, and memberships to the Nauticus Museum.

The *Iowa* and the *Wisconsin* are subject to the National Defense Act of 1996. This act includes reference to maintenance of warships to support Marine Corps operations. It specifies that the Naval Vessel Register must maintain two *Iowa*-type ships in sufficient condition to support amphibious operations. The original plan was to keep the *Iowa* and *Wisconsin* available from 2003 to 2008, during which time a system would be built to provide in-depth fire support for marines who are landing via landing craft or helicopter. But the navy has decided to put the *Wisconsin* in the hands of its present caretaker, the City of Norfolk, and remove it from the federal register by late autumn 2006.

It has been difficult to find a port or city that can properly care for the USS *Iowa*. In addition, the navy and Congress have been reluctant to put it on the list for ship donations. The battleship remains on the category B mobilization asset list and will not be available for many months for cities to bid on. Whoever takes on the ship must be able to provide monetary resources and responsible leadership. The navy does not want a repeat of the embarrassing USS *Cabot/Spanish Dedalo* fiasco or the funding problems that other memorial ships have had. Financial losses associated with these episodes violated promises to the U.S. and Spanish navies that these assets would be preserved and protected for years to come.

The *Iowa* will likely remain in a California port, as pre-ordained by legislation inaugurated by Senator Diane Feinstein (Democrat, California). The primary contenders are a private group from San Francisco and a similar group from Stockton, California. The group from San Francisco is reputedly strapped for cash, and the Stockton group has also had difficulty in aquiring the necessary backing.

It is certain that the navy will not continue to retain the *Iowa* and the *Wisconsin*, simply because of the huge expense to the taxpayers. Almost $500 million would be needed to restore the *Iowa* to active status, and a further

An overhead view of the USS *Iowa* moored next to the former *Proteus*, a submarine tender once very well known in Scotland. *Author's Collection*

$110 million to restock the ship with silken, hand-sewn gunpowder bags for the 16-inch guns. The cost is so immense because the *Iowa* has been utilized for spare parts, and Turret No. 2 has never been repaired. Studies have proven that the older ammunition bags of powder are unsafe, and a repeat of the tragedy that befell the *Iowa* in 1989 will not be risked. Even making the *Iowa* reasonably presentable by painting the upper works and superstructure, plus replacing the Burmese teak deck

with high-quality Douglas fir (with multiple coats of protective chemicals) would cost $15 to 20 million. A complete refurbishment for museum status would cost the navy over $25 million, and it is felt that these funds could better be spent in other areas of the navy. If a private group succeeds in acquiring the ship, it will have to absorb the costs for exterior painting and wooden deck replacement immediately. Also any mooring location will require expensive dredging.

At first, the *Iowa* was placed in mothballs, and its major components were sealed and protected. The now-oxidizing battleship was moored next to the USS *Wisconsin* (BB-64) in Newport, Rhode Island, until March 8, 2001, when she was hooked onto the *Sea Victory* for the forty-four-day tow to California. It seemed strange to tow the *New Jersey* from Bremerton, Washington, to the Philadelphia Naval Shipyard, and tow the *Iowa* back to the West Coast. However, when powerful politicians become involved, logic is nowhere to be found. Senator Strom Thurmond wanted the USS *New Jersey* for Camden and did not care where the *Iowa* went. Consequently, upon his orders (or strongly worded suggestion), the gun barrel training mechanisms aboard the *New Jersey* were welded closed, thus disabling the main battery, and the taxpayers paid over $4 million to move the battleships from coast to coast.

THE LONG TOW TO CALIFORNIA

The *Iowa* was towed from the East Coast of the United

A beam view of the *Iowa* shows that there has been some work on the ship. However, it appears to be from the top down, but only to the bridge deck. There is much to do, and the tarps cover work that was in progress. The top structure of the mast is stored on the aft deck, and when the *Iowa* becomes a museum, this structure will have to be re-installed through the use of a heavy lift crane. It was removed in 2001 to avoid striking bridges leading up the American River to the Sacramento Delta area. The company that was working on the ship identified a great number of structural areas requiring welds and new bracing due to rust and areas where water was trapped for long periods above deck. *Author's Collection*

The USS *New Jersey* (BB-62) prior to decommissioning and mooring in a fleet reserve location. The *New Jersey* was used heavily by the navy in World War II, Korea, and the Vietnam War. A lot of water moved under its keel during its six decades of service. The *New Jersey* was decommissioned on February 8, 1991, and was opened as a ship museum on October 15, 2001, in Camden, New Jersey. *U.S. Navy*

The USS *Wisconsin* (BB-64) moored alongside the Nauticus maritime museum in Norfolk, Virginia. The *Wisconsin* had been stricken from the navy list on January 12, 1995, and finally moved to the location at Nauticus on December 7, 2000. The ship was dedicated on April 16, 2001. The *Wisconsin* performed exceptionally well for the nation and the navy with little overt notoriety. *U.S. Navy*

The USS *Missouri* (BB-63) moored just aft of the *Arizona* Memorial in Pearl Harbor, Hawaii. There was great competition for the *Missouri* to come to San Francisco, yet Pearl Harbor won out. *Author's Collection*

States to Suisun Bay, California (just miles from San Francisco) in April 2001. One of the authors rode the towing vessel, Crowley Marine's *Sea Victory*. At one point, the tug captain and pilot allowed him to steer, thus guiding the 59,000-ton behemoth. After a few minutes and much laughter, he was told that the *Sea Victory* had been on automatic pilot!

The *Iowa* was an easy tow for the *Sea Victory* and only scraped once while transiting the locks in the Panama Canal. The battleship passed through San Francisco Bay at midnight, which was irritating to those who had been sure the battleship would be a tourist attraction along the Fisherman's Wharf area. There are those who say that the midnight tow through San Francisco Bay was the final snub to the city that has rejected the navy and the military. In actuality, the tow was arranged so that the ship could come to its new anchorage at midday, when there would be maximum light for mooring. Bringing the ship through the Golden Gate at night turned out to be wise

for another reason, too. Even with its topmast struck down on the aft part of the ship, there was still minimal room for the ship as she moved through San Pablo Bay under the toll bridges that cross the narrows.

THE *IOWA*'S FINAL BATTLE

Since 2001, the deteriorating battleship *Iowa* has still been held in reserve in Suisun Bay. But as soon as Congress enacts legislation to give the ship in-donation status and the U.S. Navy is in accord, there is a six-month window for applicants that want the ship and can prove they will financially care for her. The frontrunner has always been San Francisco (Historic Ships Memorial at Pacific Square), yet Bremerton, Washington; Long Beach, California; and now Stockton, California are expected to make very strong cases for acquiring the last of the battleships.

The San Francisco contingent has based its plan to sustain the ship on its expectation of 125,000 visitors per

A plaque aboard the USS *Missouri* shows where the Japanese and Allies signed the surrender documents ending the war in the Pacific and, in essence, the greatest war in human history. It is embedded in the deck of the *Missouri. Author's Collection*

year and an annual budget of under $4 million. From the experiences of the *Missouri, Wisconsin,* and *New Jersey,* that figure is about one-half to one-third of what will be necessary. The business managers for other battleship museums note that at least 250,000 annual visitors and an aggressive sales plan are absolutes to survive. They have the experience and know how close this kind of venture can dip into red rather than black ink.

An almost insurmountable problem with the Port of Stockton is that the area where the *Iowa* would reside

A bow shot of the USS *Iowa* at its mooring in the Suisun Bay Reserve Fleet. *Author's Collection*

is a neighborhood that time has ignored. It consists of open sulfur storage plants, gang hideouts, bars that sailors avoid, and recycling plants. The view from Interstate 5 tells it all—the area has the look of an old landfill. Despite promises to clean up the region, families will not venture through this area as it now exists to see a warship display.

The Port of Stockton does have a 6,000-foot-long pier and a deep and fresh water channel. This city is also one of the fastest-growing communities in the Central Valley of California, and the U.S. Navy has provided it with its former Rough and Ready Island facility and several modern buildings, including a 90,000-square-foot shed. The Port of Stockton has no contingency funding for acquiring and maintaining the *Iowa,* and has gone to the City of Stockton for $20 million for the startup costs. The City of Stockton has no uncommitted funding, so there is rough water ahead for all of the groups that are soliciting the battleship. Even the most naïve knows that politics and battleships make strange bedfellows!

Congressman Richard Pombo introduced legislation in 2005 to enable the *Iowa* to be donated to the Port of Stockton, but this initiative may have hurt more than helped proponents' overall plans. Unfortunately, Pombo's legislation put a stop to contracts that were to have finished painting the upper works and replaced the wooden deck of the *Iowa.* The contractor had spent only

The final tribute by the crew of the *Iowa* to their forty-seven fallen shipmates. The crew lines the railing wearing black armbands in salute and reverence for the men whose lives were taken as the result of the flareback in Turret No. 2. More than one of the men standing on deck knows that the flareback could have erupted into a catastrophic explosion which would have annihilated the entire ship. The ship is slowly moving into its homeport in Norfolk, Virginia, on April 23, 1989, four days after the accident. Turret No. 2 is stuck in its position with barrels askew and pointed to starboard. This was the position when the flareback occurred. *U.S. Navy*

$2 million of the $11.5 million needed to make the ship presentable. Work on the ship ceased months ago, and the new price tag for restarting the work is estimated to between $15 and $20 million.

Additionally, a common thread runs through every successful venture of this nature: a few good managers who are thoroughly familiar with the ship type are better than a host of highly paid consultants with little knowledge of the ship.

The fact that the *Wisconsin* has already been removed from the federal Naval Vessel Register no doubt means that the *Iowa* should have been short-listed for donation as well. The issue will be who has the resources, has prepared the necessary documents, and has plans that are certifiable and realistic. Taking on a battleship is a tremendous responsibility and a lengthy commitment not to be done lightly.

Wherever this battleship is placed, it will be appreciated just like the other memorial warships located all over the United States. The decades-old *Iowa* may be homeless for the time being, but that hopefully will change in the near future.

INDEX

General Index

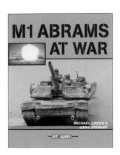

M1 Abrams At War
ISBN 0-7603-2153-1

B-17 At War
ISBN 0-7603-2522-7

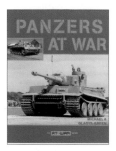

Panzers At War
ISBN 0-7603-2152-3

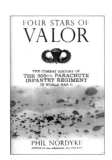

Four Stars of Valor
ISBN 0-7603-2664-9

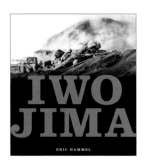

Iwo Jima
Portraits of a Battle: United States
Marines at War in the Pacific
ISBN 0-7603-2520-0

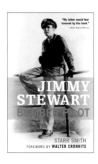

Jimmy Stewart: Bomber Pilot
ISBN 0-7603-2199-X